An Introduction into
Sociological Orientations

An Introduction into Sociological Orientations

Robert Hagedorn
University of Victoria
British Columbia, Canada

Sanford Labovitz
University of Calgary
Alberta, Canada

John Wiley & Sons, Inc.
New York   London   Sydney   Toronto

Library of Congress Cataloging in Publication Data:

Hagedorn, Robert, 1925-
An introduction into sociological orientations.

Includes bibliographical references.
1. Sociology.   2. Sociological research.
I. Labovitz, Sanford, 1935-   joint author.
II. Title. [DNLM: 1. Sociology. HM 24 L125i 1972]

HM51.H24   301'.07'2   72-7193
ISBN 0-471-33862-1

Cover: Editorial Photocolor Archives/N.Y.

Printed in the United States of America

10-9 8 7 6 5 4 3 2 1

Preface

Two deeply felt convictions resulted in the writing of this book: (1) there should be a close relationship between what is taught in introductory sociology courses and what sociologists actually do in their inquiries; and (2) college students are quite capable of handling alternate and conflicting approaches to a discipline. That is, there is no need to oversimplify a discipline like sociology by presenting only one of several different orientations to its complex subject matter. Through an understanding of the basic issues and controversial perspectives, students not only will receive a more accurate assessment of the field but will profit from the knowledge of the different approaches.

Because of these convictions, we have described the orientations in sociology as they actually are—not as we think they should be. Consequently, the inconsistencies and contradictions in the different orientations are presented as characterizations of the discipline as we perceive it. In other words, we have tried to present accurate and fair descriptions of how different sociologists approach their subject matter without making moral evaluations of how they *should* approach it.

The student will realize that the arguments among sociologists often are loud and long lasting because there is a strong tendency to believe that "my way is the right way." We caution the student not to select an approach that is most agreeable to him at this time but, instead, to closely evaluate each one, and perhaps to take a stand at a later date and try to resolve the major issues.

It is impossible to thank individually all of the students and colleagues who helped us to write this book. A few, however, made direct and substantial contributions. We are particularly grateful to Alan Hedley, Richard J. Hill, Eric Linden, and Michael Mend.

Robert Hagedorn

Sanford Labovitz

Contents

CHAPTER ONE

Substantive Orientations

Sociology is what sociologists think; or perhaps, what sociologists do; or what sociologists should do; or sociology is the study of groups or of individuals in groups; or it is the study of human behavior in general; or perhaps the study of the interaction between persons, and maybe it includes the rules and regulations of society that give form and structure to interaction; or it is the study of the acts of individuals, which includes the study of human motivation. Actually all of these phrases have been stated as "defining" the field of sociology. Their differences and complexity point to the problem of adequately defining the discipline in a few choice words.

PROBLEMS IN DEFINING SOCIOLOGY

How, then, do sociologists respond when asked, "What is sociology?" A rather typical response is to cite one definition out of many and perhaps to defend it loosely with some mis-givings about its accuracy and limited or vague scope. Such a definition may be defended on the grounds that it gives the student more direction than no definition at all. The student (before, during, or after the introductory course) may also have difficulty in defining the field. He will be likely, however, to cite a single definition of sociology if asked, and experience the same discomfort as sociologists in this situa-tion, or he may decline to define the field (as do some mem-bers of the discipline), and sum it all up by saying, "Beats me."

But is it necessary to define completely a discipline in a few choice words? Sociologists have been able to live with the fact that there is no single acceptable definition without losing their jobs, their heads, their sense of humor, or even their introductory sociology course. At this stage in the development of sociology perhaps it is best not to accept prematurely a single definition. With a somewhat broad and loose definition, the field can branch out in many directions. Besides, the definitional problem applies to many fields other than sociology without having resulted in their demise.

Indicating the scope of sociology is difficult, because its members study many things in many different ways. Nonethe-less, some indication of the breadth of a discipline is impor-tant, because it provides an initial glimpse of the method and content of its inquiry.

The purpose of this chapter is to indicate the extent of this diversity and provide a basis for reasonably defining sociol-ogy. Such a definition should retain the fundamental differ-ences, as well as similarities, that exist among sociologists.

To accomplish this goal, the chapter is divided into two sections. The first section presents the subject matter of sociology (what sociologists study), which is discussed in terms of three major substantive orientations. The second section is concerned with some current trends in sociology. By the end of the chapter you should not only have some understanding of what sociologists do, but also a knowledge of some of the basic issues in the field and some reasons for the diversity and disagreement among sociologists them-selves.

Sociologists study individual behavior and attitudes, motives or subjective states of individuals, interaction among individuals and groups, rates of human behavior (such as the suicide rate, divorce rate, and average family size), and components of the social structure. The choice of concepts or variables, the method of study, and theoretical treatment partially depend on the general substantive orientation or frame of reference of the sociologist.

THE NATURE OF SUBSTANTIVE ORIENTATIONS

A substantive orientation specifies the major parts of the world that are most relevant for study. On the bases of tradition (what sociologists say) and research (what sociologists do), the orientations of sociology may be conceptualized along three somewhat independent dimensions: (1) the *structural orientation,* which is based on the study of the structural components of groups, that is, external social factors that are assumed to influence the behavior of individuals and groups;[1] (2) the *social action orientation,* which is based on the study of the motivations and behavior of individuals in social situations—motivations refer to subjective intentions underlying an individual's action;[2] and (3) the *behavioral interaction orientation,* which is based on the study of behavioral interaction patterns among individuals—that is, the patterns of reciprocal give and take between two or more persons.[3] Most sociologists may be classified along

[1] Many of these ideas were formulated by Emile Durkheim around the turn of the century. See especially his, *The Rules of Sociological Method,* Sarah A. Solovay and John H. Mueller (translators), Glencoe, Illinois: Free Press, 8th edition, 1938, pp. 1–46; and *The Division of Labor in Society,* George Simpson (translator), Glencoe, Illinois: Free Press, 1933, pp. 1–132.

[2] Many of these ideas were expressed by Max Weber in the early part of the 20th century. See especially his, *The Theory of Social and Economic Organization,* A. M. Henderson and Talcott Parsons (translators), Oxford University Press, 1947, pp. 87–112.

[3] Perhaps the earliest proponent in sociology to bring these ideas together was Georg Simmel. See especially *The Sociology of Georg Simmel,* Kurt H. Wolff (translator), New York: Crowell-Collier, 1950.

one or more of these orientations, and the three together encompass almost all of what sociologists say about their discipline.

Structural Orientation

A traditional and prevalent orientation in sociology may be labeled structural. In its most general conception, it refers to a set of factors, characteristics, dimensions, or variables that exist in society independent of individuals, and that are imputed to constrain them to behave and think in particular ways. That is, it is assumed that individuals experiencing the same "structure" will behave in the same way. Besides its imputed influence on individual behavior, it is assumed that certain parts of the structure affect other parts.

The structural orientation may emphasize any of four related perspectives. First, the *ecological* perspective refers to societal factors such as technology, natural resources, and demographic composition (population size and density, sex ratio, family size, fertility ratio, death rate, and migration patterns). To illustrate, people in dense populations may belong to more community associations than those in less dense populations, and people in highly industrialized areas tend to have lower fertility rates than those in less industrialized areas.

A second perspective refers to society as a *network of interdependent positions.* These positions are seen as being "out there" and independent of any individual. Although people may come and go, for example, the positions of president or student remain. In this view, persons carry out the duties and obligations that are attached to their positions and interact with those in other positions. For example, physicians and patients interact in predictable patterns with the physician being dominant.

A third perspective refers more directly to the form or makeup of groups, that is, *group structure.* It includes such factors as the communication system, authority structure, group size, power, and the division of labor (that is, persons specializing in various tasks). A study of a large automobile plant, of a university, or of a jury are examples of this perspective.

Finally, structure may refer to the standards of conduct that influence persons in their behavioral and thought patterns, that is, *normative structure.* In this view, societies and groups have certain rules, laws, and customs that are followed by most of its members; and, if people do not follow these standards, they are penalized in some way. For example, in most societies, persons are not supposed to have sexual relations with certain close relatives.

The structural orientation is not unique to sociology. "Structural statements" are used often by people in their everyday lives. Young people who maintain that one should never trust anyone over 30 are implicitly assuming that regardless of individual characteristics (such as personality or conviction), there is something about passing this age that constrains people to behave in a certain way. In fact, a structural argument may be used to support this lack of trust. By the age of 30, most people are well integrated into society. They are out of school and have been working in an occupation for a few years. Most are married, are in or are supporting a family, and have accumulated some material goods. In short, they are closely tied to the established society, and have something to lose by criticizing it or changing it. They are, moreover, entrenched in a web of relationships that further constrain them to behave in "respectable" and predictable ways.

Another illustration of a structural statement is found in the frequently used question, "What do you do?", which is asked usually in initial encounters. Literally, this is a fairly ridiculous question (people brush their teeth, dress themselves, go to movies, take showers, sleep, for instance) but most people know what it means. We are asking for a person's occupation; and we are imputing to it a dominant influence on his life style. Upon finding out a person's occupation, we adjust our behavior in accordance with specified expectations. We are not likely to tell ribald jokes to a priest, and we may feel uneasy in the presence of a powerful figure like a Queen or a President.

Actually, the structural orientation may be used in two rather distinct ways that can be stated as basic sociological assumptions. The first assumption stipulates that a specific structure of society determines its other structural characteristics. For example, democratic societies tend to have many interest groups. Karl Marx suggested that capitalistic countries are likely to experience one economic crisis after another.[4] Capitalistic countries, he argued, are characterized by the profit motive, and workers receive only a minimum subsistence wage. Profits are plowed back into the corporation and production increases rapidly. But workers, he argued, are not paid enough to buy the products. This situation leads to an economic crisis like a financial depression.

The second assumption is oriented toward the structural constraints on individual behavior rather than on the characteristics of society. People from cities behave differently than those from rural areas; proletariats are the revolutionary class because of their relationship to the economic structure; and individuals in certain positions like physicians or lawyers are likely to wield greater personal power than foremen or streetcar conductors. Occupation, the last example, is often used by sociologists as an important determiner of behavior and in its extreme form may be summed up in such statements as, "the office makes the man" and "bank presidents are conservative."

Another example of the structural effect on individual behavior is the relation between type of industrial organization and worker alienation. In a detailed study of four industrial environments—a print shop, a textile mill, an automobile plant, and a chemical continuous-process operation—Robert Blauner found different degrees of powerlessness, meaninglessness, self-estrangement, and isolation, which he defined

---

[4] For a more detailed commentary see Mundell Morten Bober, *Karl Marx's Interpretation of History*, Cambridge: Harvard University Press, 1927; and Karl Marx, *Capital (translated* from the 3rd German edition by Samuel Moore and Edward Aveling; edited by Frederick Engles; revised according to the 4th German edition by Ernest Untermann), New York: The Modern Library, 1936.

as four separate types of alienation.[5] He found, furthermore, that the type of industrial setting influenced an individual's opportunity to learn and advance, and even affected his personality development.

Each of Blauner's four types of alienation was manifested in a different form and degree of intensity in each industrial setting. He found that although bureaucratic industries tend to have alienating characteristics, a particular organization's structure (its technological base, social division of labor, economic structure, and social organization) may counteract such tendencies or increase them. Workers in some industrial settings, consequently, may be highly alienated in all four dimensions while workers in other settings may feel that they have a say in the organization, that it is meaningful to them, and that they are well integrated in its structure. Workers in the automobile plant tended to be most alienated, while workers in the print shop and the chemical plant tended to be least alienated. It was difficult to reach general conclusions for all workers and for each type of alienation in each of these settings. Blauner does suggest, however, that alienation was low in the early craft stage of industry; it reached a peak in the assembly-line industries, and is declining in continuous-process industries (like the chemical plant).

A final example of the structural orientation is taken from a study by Strodtbeck et al. on jury leadership and deliberation.[6] In an experiment in which they set up mock jury trials, they found that leadership and participation in jury deliberations depended to a large extent on a person's sex and social status. Specifically, males and members of high prestige occupations were much more likely to be chosen as leaders and to participate more in discussion than were females and members of lower status occupations.

[5] Robert Blauner, *Alienation and Freedom*. Chicago: University of Chicago Press, 1964.

[6] Fred L. Strodtbeck, Rita M. James, and Charles Hawking, "Social Status in Jury Deliberations," in Eleanor E. Maccoby *et al.* (editors), *Readings in Social Psychology*, New York: Holt, Rinehart and Winston, 1958, pp. 379–388.

Social Action Orientation

In contrast to the structural orientation, the notion of social action focuses more directly on the individual. Individual acts and subjective intentions are the crucial problems for study. Subjective intentions include the ways in which persons think, feel, believe, and are motivated. The essential idea in the social action orientation is that an individual's act only can be understood and predicted by knowing how he feels about and perceives his situation. If, for example, we want to predict and understand the action of students in a classroom situation, it is first necessary to find out what motivates them by ascertaining how they feel and think and what they believe about the situation. Students who feel that what goes on in the classroom is nonsense may study a minimum amount, seldom participate in discussions, and be prone to cheat on examinations. Those with a positive attitude toward the classroom (those who perceive it as a useful learning situation) may study harder, participate more in discussions, and have fewer absences.

This orientation is quite prevalent among contemporary sociologists and is sometimes referred to as "social action theory." It was formulated early in the discipline's development by Max Weber. Weber maintained that the proper domain for sociology is the study of social action, which is behavior motivated toward specific goals and satisfying human wishes, attitudes, or dispositions. In Weber's own words, "Sociology . . . is a science which attempts the interpretive understanding of social action . . . to arrive at a causal explanation of its course and effects." Action is social only when subjective meanings are attached to the behavior of individuals. The individual, he argued, is the sole carrier of meaningful conduct, because only he can attach subjective meanings or motives to behavior. The social scientist can impute motives to individuals and thereby go beyond just predicting human behavior; he can also "understand" it. Such "understanding" is not involved in the physical sciences where the subjective states of the things investigated are not relevant.

Some everyday statements that typify this approach are: "I know how she feels because I have gone through it"; "I understand his depression because I too have worked on an assembly line"; "I know how he felt when he committed suicide after losing a loved one"; and "I once lost my job, so I can understand the feelings of those who are forced to retire." Knowing how another person feels, because you can "experience" or feel the effects of his situation, is implicit in such statements as "people are on relief because they are too lazy to work," "anyone can succeed if they really try," "a good teacher cares about his students," "you are as old as you feel," and "he is a good salesman because he is aggressive." Contrast this last statement with "he is aggressive because he is a salesman," which is a structural argument implying that there is something about being a salesman that makes people aggressive. The social action examples express the theme that subjective states of individuals are basic for understanding their acts. A large percentage of sociological research on delinquency, attitudes, company morale, job satisfaction, and social values stems from the social action orientation.

In addition to subjective intentions, social action also stresses the importance of the situation and the choices available to a person. All action, which is goal oriented, occurs in a situation, which includes conditions and alternative means that are meaningful to the individual. The conditions include the physical setting (such as the tools in a repair shop) and the social setting (such as the presence of the foreman and customers, and the rules governing interaction). The individual often has a choice of means to use in a given situation.[7] To illustrate, the worker confronted with a difficult customer can try to solve the difficulty himself, or he may call in the foreman to handle it, or he may quit his job altogether. A person who has lost someone he loves or who has lost his life savings has the unenviable choice of trying

---

[7] For a more detailed discussion of these aspects, see Alfred R. Lindesmith and Anselm L. Strauss, *Social Psychology,* 3rd edition, New York: Holt, Rinehart and Winston, 1968, Chapter 1.

to cope with the situation by himself, or seeking psychiatric help, or, perhaps, committing suicide.

An early example of the social action orientation was presented by Weber in his analysis of the relationship between the religious and economic institutions in society.[8] He made an extensive historical study of world religions and economic orders. One of his major conclusions was that the ethical code of the Puritans in the early United States gave rise to its form of capitalism. He based this conclusion on his judgment that the personal values, attitudes, motives, and feelings instilled in the American people by the Protestant ethic were conducive to and in fact produced a profit-oriented business economy. The content of their religious training motivated these people to behave in a certain way in acquiring goods and earning a livelihood.

The capitalistic economic order, Weber argued, requires certain individual characteristics for its inception and growth. One dominant and necessary value is a stress on individualism—on doing things for yourself and working for yourself. Other values necessary for a capitalistic system are hard work, thrift, self-discipline, initiative, and rationality. By acting in accordance with these values people become profit oriented and are able to develop economic enterprises.

The Puritans, Weber argued, believed that certain individuals were born among the elect, that is, among God's favored and chosen. Being among the elect, consequently, was beyond one's personal control, since this status was fixed at birth. Puritans also believed that no living person could ever know whether he was chosen or not, but that a good indicator of this status was whether he was successful in his "calling." One's calling came to be defined as one's work or business, and each individual alone had to seek God's grace by succeeding in his calling. According to Weber, no individual could, by his own acts, bring about his salvation or damnation. The best he could do is discover

[8] Max Weber, *The Protestant Ethic and the Spirit of Capitalism,* Talcott Parsons (translator), New York: Scribner's, 1958 (originally published in German in 1904–1905).

clues to his fate. By trying to be successful, which is one clue indicating membership among the elect, the Puritan came to value hard work, self-discipline, the rejection of worldly pleasures, and the achievement of righteous success in this world. Other important values among Puritans were personal initiative, acquisitiveness, individualism, and competitiveness. All of these values, according to Weber, were favorable for the emergence of a capitalistic economic order. In effect, Weber was saying that it is the values held by individuals, the subjective definitions of work, savings, and the "calling" that determine the economic structure.

If religious ethics are interpreted as social norms and social norms are considered structural, then Weber would be classified as a structuralist rather than as an action theorist. Weber, however, treats norms in a very different way than would a structuralist. A structuralist treats norms as abstractions that exist independently of individuals but constrain them to think and behave in specified ways. Certain orthodox Jews, to illustrate, are not allowed to eat any part of a pig. The social norm, according to a structuralist, that pigs are forbidden as food constrains such people to avoid them. No mention is made of how an orthodox Jew interprets the social norm or what motivates him to follow it.

In contrast, Weber's treatment of religious ethics (religious norms) specifies a personal attachment. These ethics must be meaningful to the individual. To be meaningful, they must become part of him in the sense that he accepts them internally as real and important. To determine the effects of social norms on behavior, an action theorist must find out how they are meaningful to the individual. In the case of the orthodox Jew, it is important to determine the subjective meanings and feelings he has toward the food taboo on pigs. This treatment of social norms sharply differentiates an action theorist from a structuralist. It is in the differential *treatment,* consequently, that categorizes social norms as structural or as social action.

An orientation that is compatible with Weber's social action (and can be considered a subtype of it) is the school of thought labeled *symbolic interaction.* The similarity between the two is that both stress the way people define the actions of others in terms of subjective meanings. Perhaps the major difference between the two orientations is an emphasis by followers of symbolic interaction on language and gesture as crucial aspects of human communication. The images people have of one another is considered the reality of social life; such images are based on the process of symbolic interaction.[9]

In essence, this approach assumes that an individual's personality, self-identity, human nature, personal beliefs and behavior on the one hand and society's structure and order, on the other, are products of interaction between symbolically communicating human beings. According to Tamotsu Shibutani, for example, "the direction taken by a person's conduct is seen as something that is constructed in the reciprocal give and take of interdependent men who are adjusting to one another."[10] The social structure and its cultural aspects, furthermore, are derived from such human interaction.

The closeness of this orientation to social action can be seen in its focus on the subjective meanings of individuals that define reality. A famous statement on "the definition of the situation" by W. I. Thomas (one of the first symbolic interactionists) typifies this orientation. He claimed that "if men define the situation as real, it is real in its consequences."[11] The terms, then, of interaction are similarly defined in these two groups. The main difference lies in the stress on symbols as the source of human nature.

In contrast to the structural orientation, which views a group's culture as external to and imposing on individuals, the symbolic interaction orientation treats culture as comprised of appropriate thought and behavior that develop out of the communication process. The emphasis of symbolic interactionists is on how culture develops, on the individual's

---

[9] An early formulation of this orientation was Charles Horton Cooley. See *Human Nature and the Social Order*, Scribner's, 1902.

[10] *Society and Personality*, Englewood Cliffs, New Jersey: Prentice-Hall, p. 23.

[11] *The Child in America*, New York: Knopf, 1928, p. 572.

internalization of culture, and on the standardized patterns of interaction.

A follower of this approach stresses the importance of the socialization process, in which a person develops self-aware-ness and self-identity, and, consequently, becomes a social human being. Self-awareness and self-conception are based on how others treat a person in their mutual interaction. George Herbert Mead (another early developer of this ap-proach) saw this process as role-taking or "taking the role of the other," in which persons become human by learning the social roles, expectations, rules, and regulations of society.[12] Charles Horton Cooley's concept of "looking-glass self" also fits this orientation.[13] This concept is concerned with a person's orientation toward himself in terms of posi-tive or negative self-identity. This self-orientation reflects the manner in which he is treated and judged by others; if he believes in the treatment and judgment, then these become real in their consequences for him. There are, Cooley argued, three phases that each person goes through in developing self-awareness: (1) he imagines how he appears to others, (2) he imagines how others judge him, and (3) he reacts emotionally with pride or mortification to the imputed judgment of others.

If Mead and Cooley and the other symbolic interactionists are correct, an individual's self-awareness (whether he con-ceives of himself as popular or unpopular, good or bad, bright or dull, pretty or plain) depends on his perception of how others think of him and treat him. They argue, further-more, that a person is generally correct in his imputed judg-ment of how he is perceived and treated by others.

As an example, consider a hypothetical suicide. If individ-uals evaluate themselves as they perceive others evaluating them, the crucial variable in suicide is the response of others. If a businessman continually fails in his endeavors by going into debt or by losing his business, he will experience shame

---

[12] *Mind, Self, and Society, Chicago:* The University of Chicago Press, 1934.

[13] Charles Horton Cooley, footnote 9.

in his interaction with others. He will impute negative judgments of himself to his wife, relatives, colleagues, and co-workers, and this negative emotion is an imputed reason for his suicide.

To test these notions, Miyamoto and Dornbusch conducted an experimental study of self-awareness.[14] They divided their subjects into several small groups and after a period of interaction asked each subject (with regard to four characteristics) to (1) rate himself, (2) rate the others in the group, (3) rate himself as he perceives others in the group would rate him, and (4) rate himself as he perceives others in general would rate him. The characteristics to be rated were intelligence, self-confidence, physical attractiveness, and likableness. The results of the study were consistent with the symbolic interactionist point of view. Subjects in general rated themselves as others rated them and as they perceived others would rate them. The results support the thesis that a person's conception of himself is based on how others perceive and treat him in everyday interaction.

Behavioral Interaction Orientation

A third school of thought states that the proper area of study for sociology is the overt (observable) patterns of behavior occurring in interpersonal relations; this is the behavioral interaction orientation. The emphasis is on what individuals and human groups do in behaving with and to one another, rather than on their subjective states or motivations. A behavioral interactionist focuses on establishing the patterns of behavior of interacting persons.

A person's everyday life is comprised of a wide variety of patterns of interaction. In dating, for example, the behavior of the interacting persons takes on definite and quite predictable patterns. These patterns depend on such personal characteristics as manipulative skill, social status, and the degree to which one individual dominates. A skillful male (in

---

[14] S. Frank Miyamoto and Sanford Dornbusch, "A Test of Interactionist Hypotheses of Self-Conception," *American Journal of Sociology, 61* (March, 1956), pp. 399–403.

the more traditional relationship) can present a believable "line" to his date for sexual favors; a skillful female can manipulate her date to take her to expensive places. The person least involved in the relation, that is, the one who likes the other less or is less committed to the relationship, is very likely to dominate on dates; they will go where she demands or do what he wants. Dates between a wealthy girl and a poor guy may prove embarrassing for both, and are likely to be dominated by the girl.

In a classroom situation, the difference in status between student and teacher produces predictable patterns of inter-action. If a student asks a question, the teacher may say it is irrelevant, may misinterpret it, or just ignore it; the teacher controls the interaction to a large extent; it is doubtful that a student can behave in a similar manner when the teacher asks him a question. The student is required to answer the question, which is assumed to be relevant simply because the teacher did the asking. A student who does ignore the question is likely to feel repercussions: he may fail the course, or be kicked out, or may even be shunned by fellow students.

People usually become very adept at predicting patterns of interaction, which may well be the most important device for holding societies together. We can fairly accurately antici-pate the responses of others in certain situations and, there-fore, can adjust our behavior accordingly. This simplifies our lives considerably and produces at least some degree of harmony between persons. A nearly universal reaction that leads to predictable friendly and unfriendly interaction pat-terns is: my friend's friend is my friend, my friend's enemy is my enemy, my enemy's friend is my enemy and my enemy's enemy is my friend. To be able to anticipate someone's behavior, we implicitly assume that people behave like they have before in similar situations, that there is constancy or patterns in human behavior. We generally know, for example, how our spouse or parents will respond to our behavior. In more traditionalist families, a husband who comes home from the office late and with an unfamiliar shade of lipstick on his shirt is likely to find an angry wife; and a student who does not study or receives poor grades is not likely to reap bountiful rewards from his parents.

Since much of our life consists of interacting with others, it should hardly be surprising that a scientific field that concentrates on the description and explanation of predictable patterns of interaction has developed. Interaction is such a prevalent concept for most sociologists that it is included in the definition of some of its major divisions: for example, society, groups, formal organization, and the family.

One of the early exponents of this perspective was Georg Simmel, who defined sociology in terms of the study of patterns of interaction or "forms-of-sociation." Treating them as abstractions, Simmel felt that interaction patterns could be determined in all aspects of social life: for example, in the political, religious, and economic institutions of society. In attempting to establish patterns of interaction, Simmel wrote extensively on such subjects as the stranger, social conflict, and city life. In summary, the basic unit of analysis for Simmel was not the individual, but the behavioral interaction patterns between individuals.

According to Simmel, two basic conceptual abstractions are the dyad, an interacting pair, and the triad, an interacting three-person group. The dyad, according to Simmel, is the simplest association, but it contains the ingredients of material for the more complex forms. When two individuals interact, one may dominate the other, or the pattern may be equalitarian. In the interaction patterns subsumed under coquetry (flirting), for example, the association is based on offer and refusal between male and female. The basic pattern revolves around the elusive promises of the female, who rejects the male but never deprives him of hope; she vacillates between yes and no and, consequently, holds out the hope of acquiescence. Coquetry is complimentary to both persons and is exemplified by brief cocktail party flirtations. It should be recognized that once a decision has been reached, the pattern of interaction changes. It may be the beginning of a secret romance or the end of a brief encounter. This rather superficial form of repartee may thus lead to a somewhat more serious and deep but still "playful" form of interaction.

If a third party enters a relationship (the triad), the patterns of interaction may change dramatically. The third person may choose sides and upset the balance of the dyadic relation, or he may become a mediator in resolving conflict between the two. In an informal discussion, a single individual is disadvantaged when confronted by two who oppose his position. In a formally set up boxing match, the referee has broad powers to control the behavior of the fighters.

Caplow has extended some of Simmel's ideas in considering the tendency for traids to divide into coalitions, that is, two members uniting against a third.[15] Which members join into a coalition, he maintains, is predictable from knowledge of the distribution of power. For example, if three children, Bill, John, and Dick, are playing and Bill is stronger than both John and Dick, if John and Dick are equal in strength, and if John and Dick combined are stronger than Bill, then the predictable coalition is John and Dick against Bill.

In his discussion of "the stranger," Simmel was concerned with patterns of interaction characteristic of this type of person. He maintained, for example, that traders and traveling salesmen, who went from town to town where they were not well known, would not only have predictable economic transactions with the town's people, but would also share in some of their itimate secrets. Many people were willing to tell them town scandals and personal secrets that they would not tell to intimate friends or close relations. Perhaps they felt the stranger was "safe" since his stay was brief, and one did not have him as a "knowing" neighbor. Some townspeople, furthermore, could identify with the characteristics they shared with the stranger: for example, his occupation, his social standing, and his ethnicity. Such identification, according to Simmel, formed the basis for allowing the person to confide in the stranger.

In the following studies illustrating behavioral interaction, it should be noted that the researchers are not content with describing patterns of interaction. They also want to explain their nature and occurrence. This concern with explanation treats interaction patterns as dependent variables. A depen-

---

[15] Theodore Caplon, *Two Against One*, New Jersey: Prentice Hall, 1968.

dent variable is the effect or what is being explained or predicted. The independent variable, in contrast, is the cause (of
the dependent variable) or what is being used to do the
explaining or the predicting. In each of the following examples
the independent variable is stated first; the dependent second: status integration is negatively related to suicide;
urbanization causes delinquency; social class is directly
related to community involvement.

An interesting study that demonstrates the behavioral interaction orientation is an experiment on the effects of the
formal structure of small groups by Alex Bavelas.[16] Bavelas
set up three different communication patterns to study their
effects on group performance, leadership, and morale. His
three patterns can be diagramed as follows:

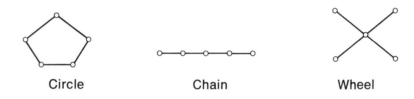

Circle   Chain   Wheel

In the circle each position is directly linked to two neighbor-
ing positions and indirectly linked to two more remote positions. In the chain, only the three middle positions are directly
linked to two others; the two end positions are directly linked
to one other; and the central position is the only one which is
one step removed from the two ends. The middle position,
consequently, is most centrally located, while its two neigh-
boring positions are more centrally located than the two
ends. Finally, the wheel has one central position directly
linked to the other four, and each of the other four positions
is linked directly only to the central position. The wheel has
a more centrally located position than the chain; and the
chain has a more centrally located position than the circle.

[16] "Communication Patterns in Task-Oriented Groups," in Dorwin
Cartwright and Alvin Zander (Eds.), *Group Dynamics*, New York: Harper
and Row, 1969, pp. 503–511.

Bavelas sent a series of groups containing five persons each into these three patterns with the task of solving a problem of locating a common symbol for each member. Of six different symbols ($\bigcirc$, $\triangle$, *, $\square$, +, $\Diamond$), and each member had five, of which only one was common to all. By communicating through cubicles, which directly and indirectly linked persons to others according to the three patterns, the problem was generally solved. Persons communicated by sending written notes to one another if they were directly linked. An experimenter kept track of the messages and the time required to solve the problem; and immediately after the experiment each subject was given a questionnaire. One of the major conclusions of the study is that the individual occupying the most central position in a pattern was more likely to be designated leader of the group. Morale, furthermore, was lowest for those in the peripheral positions. Finally, individuals in the chain and the wheel required less time on the average than those in the circle to solve the problem.

Closely related to the behavioral interaction orientation is social exchange theory, as espoused by George C. Homans.[17] Homans emphasizes a model for explaining social interaction, which is based on certain psychological and economic considerations. The major proposition of exchange theory is that every human interaction is an exchange of goods and services. Interaction does not endure unless there is a "profit" for both parties. Two individuals will continue to interact as long as it is beneficial to both. The profits of an exchange consist of the differences between its social rewards and its social costs.

An example of a persistent pattern of interaction explained by exchange theory is the classroom situation where students and teacher meet on a regular basis. Since the pattern covers a set period of time (a quarter, a semester, an academic year) and then terminates, exchange theory must specify the profits accrued during the interaction period and show that termination accompanies the extinction of such profits for both

[17] *Social Behavior: Its Elementary Forms,* New York: Harcourt, Brace and World, 1961.

student and teacher. The profits for the teacher include remuneration (pay) and the personal rewards of teaching. Even in a rather "dull" and nonresponsive class, the teacher is likely to finish the term. It would not be profitable for him to quit, because he not only loses income but possibly his job and therefore his prestige. Not only is the cost of the classroom situation probably less for the student but so is the cost of quitting. The student receives the rewards of academic credit, learning, and perhaps sheer enjoyment of the lectures and the text. Compared with the teacher, he is not as tied to the class by financial considerations, and he has readily available alternatives if he quits. He could, for example, make up credits in the following term, and if he quits early enough in the term the economic cost is usually minimal. If this analysis is correct, exchange theory suggests that it is more likely for a student than a teacher to quit a particular class.

Some Implications of the Three Orientations

It is often necessary to distinguish between the independent and dependent variables in a study; and it is especially important if an attempt is made to explain or establish the causes of some event or phenomenon. If a causal model is considered, the independent variable is the causal factor that produces the effect or dependent variable. It is therefore assumed that the independent (or explanatory) variable occurs first or changes prior to the dependent variable. Some physicians, for example, consider smoking (the independent variable) to be the cause of lung cancer (the dependent variable or the effect). If a study is not derived from a causal model, the independent variable may be assumed only to change first and not cause a change in the dependent variable. Under this condition independent and dependent variables are only considered to be related or to covary in some manner.

The three major orientations in sociology can be distinguished by their emphasis on different independent and dependent variables. Behavioral interactionists usually emphasize interaction between individuals as the dependent variable or the effect. Interaction, consequently, defines the field of sociology and is the major type of variable to be explained. An interactionist usually does not clearly state the independent variables, those factors that cause or explain particular types of interpersonal interaction. He may, however, look to structural (for example, ecological factors, positions, group makeup, or norms) or social action variables (for example, motivation) to explain the interaction. The superordinate-subordinate relation between father and son may be explained, for example, by the family structure in a society (structural orientation) or by the way family members perceive and define the nature of the relation (social action orientation).

Followers of the social action orientation usually focus on subjective states as the independent or explanatory variable. To explain a suicide or a murder or one person's hatred for another, the researcher may scrutinize the subjective states of the individual to determine his motives and the way he perceives the situation. He may find, for example, that the person defines the situation as hopeless after a business failure, or after discovering that another person is having an affair with his wife.

In contrast to these two orientations, for a structuralist the independent variable always is assumed to be structural, while the dependent variable may be structural, social action, or interaction. To illustrate, a structuralist may turn to the capitalistic economic system to explain (1) a society's power structure, (2) the motivations of individuals to invest in stocks and bonds, and (3) the interaction between governors and visiting dignitaries. A "pure" structuralist might insist on working solely with structural variables for both the effect and the cause. That is, he might define sociology as the study of characteristics that exist independently of the individual (such as properties of whole populations or societies). His emphasis would be on explaining one structural characteristic by other structural characteristics.[18]

While the structuralist searches for explanation in the

[18] Leo F. Schnore, "The Myth of Human Ecology," *Sociological Inquiry,* *31*, (2), 1969, pp. 128–139.

characteristics of societies, a social action theorist examines the subjective intentions of actors. A structuralist would maintain that certain societal conditions constrain people to behave in certain ways and determine other characteristics of society. A basic tenet of social action, in contrast, is the insistence that the individual must be taken into account; the structure of the situation determines behavior only if the structure is perceived in a particular way by the individuals involved.

To illustrate the differences between the two, consider the issue of cheating on examinations by college students. A structuralist might attempt to explain such cheating in terms of the structure of the college, the social pressure for passing, or maybe by the structural contradictions in the system itself (such as seeming to stress learning but actually supporting athletics). Given such conditions, it may be argued, a certain proportion of students will cheat, and the only way to reduce the amount of cheating is to change the structure of the system. In contrast to the structuralist, a social action theorist would argue that cheating can be explained only if we know how students define the situation. If a student defines the situation as a learning experience and sees the examinations as true tests of learning, he will not cheat regardless of the structure of the situation. If, however, he defines the situation solely as a means to an occupation or to graduate school and thinks learning occurs independent of the classroom, he might cheat if he feels it is the only or easiest way of getting a passing grade. Such cheating will occur, furthermore, under any social structure. To reduce cheating, consequently, the individual's definition of the situation must be changed. In short, the action theorist searches for explanation in the subjective states of persons; he attempts to establish their definitions or perceptions of the social situation. The structuralist, in contrast, focuses on the social situation itself as the causal factor, and disregards individual subjective states.

Table 1 is a presentation of the three major sociological orientations with their focus on independent and dependent variables as discussed above. In addition to its concise sum-

Table 1.

Examples of the Structural, Social Action, and Interaction
Orientations by Independent and Dependent Variables

Independent Variable	Dependent Variable		
	Structural	Social Action	Behavioral Interaction
Structural	Durkheim—Division of Labor Marx—Power Structure "Economic system determines family structure."	Marx—Class Consciousness Durkheim—Suicide "A person's occupation determines his voting preference."	Simmel—Dyad and Triad "A person's social class determines his marriage partner."
Social Action	Weber—Capitalism and Religious Values "Religious values determine society's economic order."	Mead and Cooley—Self Development "A person's perception of how he is treated determines his self image."	Simmel—The Stranger "Self image determines frequency of interaction at parties."

mary, the cell entries illuminate two crucial points: (1) a sociologist may be dealing with different kinds of variables at different times, and consequently, he may be labeled a structuralist one time and a social action theorist another; and (2) the way in which the subject matter of sociology is defined depends on whether the major focus is on the independent variable, the dependent variable, or both.

An interactionist may define sociology as the study of social interaction or human interrelations. His major task, usually, is to describe or explain the nature of such interaction. A social action theorist may define sociology as the study of the subjective states of individuals and their behavior in social situations. His major task, usually, is to explain a person's act by his subjective intentions or personal motives: his perceptions and definitions of the situation. A structuralist may define sociology as the study of the social structure; its network of positions and roles, its communication and authority channels, its rules and regulations, and its persistent behavioral patterns. His major task is to explain parts of the social structure, or social action, or interaction by selected aspects of the social structure.

A combination of these three definitions of sociology may be as close as we can come to adequately defining the field. Combining the three, *sociology is the study of human interaction, social action, and social structure.*

A logical possibility, not presented in the table, is to treat interaction as an independent variable in explaining structure, social action, and interaction itself. Although this may be a possibility, sociologists seldom treat interaction as an independent variable. It should be noted that the table is not all-inclusive in other respects as well. Sociologists may use independent variables other than structure and social action to explain their subject matter. George C. Homans, as illustrated previously, attempts to explain interaction patterns partly with a model based on economic and psychological variables.

RADICAL AND BLACK SOCIOLOGY

The discussion of radical and black sociology outlines the more general characteristics of these views. Because there are exceptions to the general characteristics, some sociologists (probably those more closely associated with the radical and black movements in the field) are not likely to accept all aspects of the description. These perspectives, furthermore, are in a state of fluctuation—some of the views are recently emerging, while others are changing.

There does not seem to be a clear connection between the more traditional substantive orientations and being a radical or a black sociologist. These sociologists, consequently, may be structuralists, social action theorists, behavioral interactionists, or a combination of the three. Those who consider themselves radical or black sociologists are more concerned with the usage of sociological knowledge than with the nature of sociology. These perspectives are predominantly based on a values issue, and they revolve around the priority problem of who should be the beneficiaries of knowledge.

Although the relevance of sociology for society has been debated for years, it has become a more vocal concern over the last decade.[19] Stressing relevance and moral evaluations, the two rather loosely defined frames of reference of radical and black sociology have developed, whose advocates are a small but not insignificant number of sociologists (predominantly young, black, or both). Radical and black sociology are presented together because some of their major lines of thought are similar, though they diverge on a few important issues. It should be noted that radical and black sociologists tend to be physically separated professionally and socially, and have developed separate journals. It is somewhat debatable, consequently, whether they should be considered together. We have taken the view that presented together their similarities and differences can be highlighted. It should be noted also that not all young sociologists or black sociologists are followers of these views, and it is difficult to determine the number of sociologists with such ideas.

Over three decades ago Lynd asked the question, "Knowledge for what?", implying that knowledge for knowledge's sake was not enough and that scientific study must lead to the advancement of the community or society.[20] That is, scientific knowledge is justified only if it works for the benefit of man. Just what benefits man depends to some extent on personal values. According to some persons, a guaranteed minimum income will benefit society by increasing the health and productivity of impoverished people; while according to others it will hinder society by reducing motivation to work. Scientific research on this issue pertaining to success in business is justified only in a society that values personal achievement and acquisition. In a like manner only in an

[19] See, especially, Alvin W. Gouldner, "The Sociologist as Partisan: Sociology and the Welfare State," *American Sociologist, 3* (May, 1968), pp. 103–117; and Thomas Ford Hoult, ". . . Who Shall Prepare Himself to the Battle?" *American Sociologist, 3* (February, 1968), pp. 3–8.

[20] Robert S. Lynd, *Knowledge for What?* Princeton: Princeton University Press, 1939.

atheistic or agnostic society is scientific research on the irrationality of religion justified. Even research on the lethal aspects of cancer and the harmful effects of war require the values of prolonged life and peace before it is justified. In summary, research and knowledge is justified only if it benefits man according to certain specified values. If potential knowledge is considered harmful, like the bomb or germ warfare, then maybe, the research should not take place.

Can sociology be value free? Those favoring a value-free discipline assume that scientific evidence is independent of the researcher's values. They do not deny the existence of such values, but only contend that they can be controlled adequately in social research. Such individuals assume, furthermore, that the scientist and the citizen are distinctly separate roles, and a scientist should not take a stand on social issues. As a citizen, however, he may take a stand on important issues—he may support a particular cause and advocate change in society. They further believe that science cannot determine what ought to be, but only what is. Scientific statements cannot determine whether a value judgment is right or wrong. There is nothing about being a scientist, moreover, that gives them the moral right (compared to anyone else) to dictate policy over their discoveries. They have no more right to specify what should be done with the bomb than any other citizen.

In contrast, radical and black sociologists feel that being neutral is impossible, because taking no stand at all supports the status quo. The scientist, they may argue, has knowledge of the consequences of his discovery, which places him in a better position to argue for the "best" values.

Some radical and black sociologists assume that values enter into every stage of the research process and therefore cannot be separated from science. Objectivity is denied. How a person observes behavior, how he conceptualizes his problem, and how he interprets his data are intimately tied to his values. Because values cannot be separated from the scientist in his studies, social science is "subjective" in nature.

This position on values and science is not advocated by all those labeled radical or black. Some are not antiscience.

They are concerned rather with the problems of the masses of people and wish to serve their ends. They may be quite willing to use the appropriate scientific techniques in their studies. Traditionally, according to these radical and black sociologists, most sociologists have studied what were seen as problems by the wealthy and the powerful, and researching these problems served the ends of such elites. According to this view, sociologists should not remain the Uncle Toms of the ruling class.

In reaction to the conservative notion of maintaining the status quo, advocators of radical sociology have changed Lynd's "knowledge for what?" question to "knowledge for whom?". Sociologists following the radical and black perspectives answer this question by stating that knowledge should be for the oppressed. The oppressed either refers predominantly to the impoverished and powerless groups in society (according to most radical sociologists) or to blacks (according to most black sociologists).

The frames of reference of radical and black sociologists can be subsumed under four major points: (1) opposition to the existing orientation of "establishment" sociologists and their emphasis on particular methods, (2) accepting a radical political orientation and acting to change conditions in society, (3) focusing on concepts that are contemporarily meaningful to persons in an emotional and historical sense, and (4) employing a conflict model of society.

Radical and black sociologists take an anti-establishment point of view toward society. They consider social scientists to be traditional and conscious or unconscious supporters of the existing social order. Social scientists, some argue, are employed by the major institutions of society. They teach in its colleges or universities or carry out research in its private business enterprises or governmental institutions. Such institutions pay their salaries, which provides them with material goods. But in exchange the institutions require obedience and support. While radical sociologists are against establishment sociology, black sociologists claim to be against white sociology, which they feel supports the existing white-dominated social order.

Social scientists often receive large sums of money for research from large public and private institutions. Such research grants, according to radical and black sociologists, require the social scientist to carry out investigations only in areas stipulated by the granting institutions. Research based upon these large grants, therefore, necessarily supports the status quo or existing social order. Social scientists must conform to the dictates of the social order to be awarded these grants; and those receiving such grants are more likely to receive a higher salary, travel more extensively, and be promoted to higher ranks in their institutions than those who do not. It is therefore imperative to conform and not to shake the existing social structure in order to receive the major rewards as defined by society. A further implication is that the social scientist must be pro-establishment and, therefore, biased in his research. If he comes up with "negative" findings about the establishment, he is not likely to receive additional grants and societal rewards.

The antiscientific attitude of some of the radical and black sociologists is based on the notion that social phenomena are different from physical phenomena; consequently, the methods of science are not applicable. Social scientists do more than study the social system; they think, reflect, and interact with it, and thereby change it. Under these circumstances, prediction and explanation of social phenomena are trivial. Consistent with some traditional sociologists, they do not think it is proper to "study" people.

The second major consideration of these perspectives is that many radical and black sociologists advocate change in society and, of course, advocate a radical political orientation. They feel that the direction of change in society is influenced by the political orientation of the scientists. Traditional sociologists support the status quo, while radical and black sociologists advocate and work for changes. In fact, the emphasis seems to be more on changing society than on understanding it or explaining relations. All social scientists take a stand, whether they are aware of it or not; radical and black sociologists make their political orientations explicit.

In their political orientations, many black sociologists feel they should designate a course of action for black people in the United States. The course of action should be oriented toward liberation either (1) on a pluralistic basis, that is, by establishing a separate but powerful culture, but remaining in the country, or (2) by migration, that is, by establishing a separate nation (most often designated as a country or countries in Africa, but sometimes stated as taking over a few states and seceding). A third alternative of integration is not acceptable, and is undoubtedly felt to hinder rather than promote liberation.

The conceptual framework of these views, the third major point, is based on an antiestablishment political action orientation. Although the realities in society are power relations, the oppression of the poor and/or black, and the inherent conflict among groups, sociologists, as some argue, insist on such "watered down" (in terms of emotional and historical meaning) concepts as authority, authoritarianism, and competition for analytical and descriptive purposes. These latter concepts are not adequate to meet the problems in society, and they express conservative values. Under this notion, concepts should be based on subjectivity and tied to human history. They should be relevant to the contemporary problems of society as well as meaningful to its people and based on their emotions. Finally, concepts should not be oriented to objectivity and measurability, but should have heuristic value.

Because of the emphasis on historical meaning and current reality, such standard concepts as prejudice and discrimination are not adequate for the situation in such countries as the United States. The United States, it is argued, is a racist society and should be described and analyzed as such. Racism is a more powerful and accurate concept because it captures the historical context of the overwhelming oppression. For similar reasons, a black sociologist is very likely to prefer the concepts of black or African over Negro or nonwhite, colonization over segregation, and liberation over integration. The concept of Negro may also be rejected because of its ties to slavery.

The final point refers to the class conflict model of society that is explicitly or implicitly a significant characteristic of radical and black sociology. This model stands in sharp contrast to the consensus model, which assumes that a society is primarily based on shared values and norms among its people. The consensus model is seen as an establishment sociologist's position. Societies, according to the conflict model, are comprised of groups with different interests; and one or a few groups are in the power positions and oppress all other people. According to the radical sociologists, social problems and oppression arise from exploitation by dominant groups. Such exploitation by the "haves" alienate the "have nots," who become powerless and impoverished. Basically, a rather loose to fairly strong Marxian scheme of class struggle and oppression is espoused. Some younger radical sociologists, in fact, appear to combine Marxian notions with the scientific method to aid the poor or alienated in society.

The position of the black sociologists is similar in its conflict orientation, but the emphasis is shifted to the exploitative and oppressive racist policies of the dominantly white society that has alienated blacks, and left them powerless and impoverished. While radical sociologists are likely to emphasize social class as the major variable in societal conflict (the rich as opposed to the poor, or those in power as opposed to those oppressed), blacks are likely to emphasize race as the crucial variable. Although class may be an important variable in its own right, it is the fact of being black in a white racist society that is most significant. Blacks, according to this view, have been used as an economic tool by whites since slavery in the United States and, therefore, have been alienated and economically deprived. The conflict in society, consequently, revolves primarily around race and only secondarily around class. Blacks must unite and revolt because they are black in a racist society, not because they are poor. Because of racism, blacks have developed their own culture, which unifies them as a people.

Both the radical and black perspectives advocate violent change usually in the form of revolution. The revolution, furthermore, should be now. Generally, these sociologists are willing to use the "facts" of social science to further their goals (changing conditions in society).

There appears to be a major inconsistency for some of the individuals with these perspectives. Some radical and black sociologists often play down the value of science or even the possibility of having a social science, but they want to use the facts of science (which many claim to be subjective in nature) to change society. If we cannot establish facts objectively, how can such "facts" be used to further one's ends?

Nonetheless, these perspectives have proved to be quite viable, especially among the young and black sociologists. These scientists, furthermore, have challenged some of the basic assumptions of the social scientists. The challenge could prove to be a healthy one for sociology, if it makes sociologists reconsider and reflect on the nature of their discipline.

ETHNOMETHODOLOGY

This is another orientation of recent origin that has challenged some of the traditional beliefs in sociology. Despite its rather vague perspectives and some internal disagreement, this view is viable and seems to be gaining followers.

In a general sense, ethnomethodology is a loose theoretical orientation, with some implications for restructuring traditional methodological practices. As far as investigations are concerned followers seem to favor any method that is as direct and close to the everyday life of people as possible: for example, films of people behaving "naturally," personal letters, transcripts of conversations, and participant observations. In general, they view questionnaires and interviews with disdain. Some have even criticized the use of variables in data analysis and the employment of causal analysis in theories and model building.

But it is in its theoretical orientation that ethnomethodology is attempting to present a different way of viewing the social world. Ethnomethodology is primarily concerned with the methods people use to carry out the ordinary, routine, and practical activities of their everyday lives.[21] The scientific method used by sociologists in their social inquiries, consequently, is one of the areas of study for followers of this orientation. In this view, science is a method used by sociologists in their activities of carrying out studies. The other "methods" that nonscientists use to order their lives are of equal concern to them: for example, the uses of religion, beliefs, or magic to "explain" events.

It should be noted that the following description of the ethnomethodological orientation will not be accepted in its entirety by all of its advocates (if for no other reason than there is disagreement among them). In one way or another, however, each ethnomethodologist must contend with the following three points: (1) the activities of everyday life, (2) language and meaning, and (3) the normative aspects of situations and the way people use norms.

According to the first point, ethnomethodologists emphasize the direct study of everyday life activities. These activities include interactions and communications—the way people discuss, argue, flirt, teach, learn, question, and order their world into a comprehensible form. Rather than investigating the "products" or "reflections" of activities such as occupational prestige, formal level of education, or degree of isolation, the stress is on directly observing the individual activities involved in prestige, education, or isolation. That is, studies oriented to what people actually do that may be reflected in these variables. A person may use a different kind of grammar or initiate few interactions with others, which may be reflected in occupational prestige.

The second point is the emphasis on understanding the language and meanings of the people under consideration. In this regard, it is somewhat similar to the orientations of social action and symbolic interaction, which also stress language and communication between individuals. The everyday activities of life, like arguing and questioning, can be viewed as having a grammar or form. The task of the ethno-

[21] Lindsey Churchill, "Ethnomethodology and Measurement," *Social Forces, 50* (December, 1971), pp. 182–191.

methodologist is to establish the appropriate categories and rules for such a grammar or form. To do so, one needs to understand the subtle meanings of language and how people use language in their everyday lives. One reason why its advocates look unfavorably on the use of questionnaires and interviews is that they believe the subtleties of language are not understood well enough to formulate useful questions. The only useful technique, consequently, is some form of participant observation, which requires being a member of a group so that the observer can understand what is going on. In this sense the orientation is somewhat similar to the method of *Verstehen.*

Social norms and the way people use norms (the third point) play a prominent part in ethnomethodological investigations. Briefly stated, social norms are standards that specify how people should behave. To the ethnomethodologist, norms are considered to be general and abstract. They must be interpreted by the individual in an ad hoc manner and applied to specific situations. For example, a no smoking sign in an auditorium really does not apply to the specific situation where as part of his role an actor smokes a cigarette. The general norm of no smoking must be interpreted for the specific situation. How social norms are interpreted and used by people is a major aspect for investigation.

SUMMARY

A frame of reference, point of view, or substantive orientation specifies the major aspects of the world by indicating the relevant concepts and variables for study. Three basic substantive orientations in sociology are structural, social action, and behavioral interaction. The structural orientation focuses on certain external social factors (existing in society independent of individuals) that are assumed to influence human behavior. These external social factors may be ecological (technology, natural resources, or demographic composition), interdependent positions (like physicians and patients), group makeup (like the communication system, authority structure, power relations, and division of labor), and standards of conduct (such as rules, laws, and customs).

The social action orientation, in contrast, focuses more directly on characteristics of the individual, and especially on his acts and subjective intentions. Subjective intentions include the ways persons think, feel, believe, and are motivated. The social action orientation assumes that an individual's act can be understood or explained by knowing how he feels and perceives the situation. It is essential, then, to find out what motivates a person to behave in one way rather than another.

Finally, the behavioral interaction orientation focuses on the observable patterns of behavior occurring in interpersonal relations. In contrast to the social action orientation, the emphasis is not on subjective intentions (largely covert) but on overt forms of interaction.

Two current trends are the perspectives of radical and black sociologists. Although rooted, to some extent, in the three more traditional orientations, followers of these perspectives have put a major emphasis on the relevance of sociology to the "advancement" or change of societies. Predicated on the notion that sociology should be used to help the "oppressed" rather than the elites, they advocate radical change in society, and insist that social scientists take a stand on important issues. Such changes should either help the poor (according to radical sociologists) or the black (according to black sociologists).

Finally, the recent emergence of the perspective of ethnomethodology has oriented a few sociologists to the study of the routine activities of our everyday lives. This perspective has taken root mainly on the west coast of the United States. It seems to be firmly entrenched, however, and it may influence some sociologists to reevaluate their orientations.

The above orientations illustrate how most sociologists approach their subject matter. The field of sociology is obviously characterized by a diversity of opinion. Sociology, however, has been comprehensive and broad enough to survive under these conditions, and the diversity even may be considered healthy for its development.

CHAPTER TWO

Scientific Orientations

Most everyone is concerned with explaining everyday occurrences and major historical events. Crime, riots, war, marital unhappiness, anxiety, drinking, drugs, student unrest, black power, poor study habits, middle-class "hangups," international trade, greeting forms in different countries, and poverty are just a few of the many phenomena that we try to either explain, understand, or determine the causes of.

Why is there student unrest and racial conflict in most of the "developed" and relatively wealthy countries of the world? Are these explained by an industrialized society causing alienation (powerlessness and meaninglessness) among its population, which induces some people at the bottom of the social structure to attempt to obtain power? Or are they explained by the notion that industrialized societies and their institutions (in this case, colleges and universities, and their economic orders) have not met the needs of students and the economically impoverished; and this condition has led to frustration, which in turn has led to aggression expressed in protest and riots? Or, as a third alternative, are they explained by the existence of a few radicals, revolutionists, or communists on campuses and in ghettoes who instigate and exploit students and the impoverished to unrest? Are they explained by man's supposed instinctual hatred for people different from him; a hatred for those in other groups? Finally, can they be explained by considering them to be necessary for the survival of industrialized societies, because they maintain their vitality by keeping their people alert? You may believe and accept any one or all of these as the true explanation. But which one is correct? Could they all be wrong or all be right? How can you tell?

Before such events are explained there is a more basic problem of establishing them as facts. That is, have they "in fact" occurred? Have they occurred in the manner you have perceived them? Could they be figments of the imagination, dreamed up by a few individuals who are overly concerned? Is there really student unrest and racial strife? If there are such events, how prevalent are they? Do they represent just a few vocal radicals or very large but, perhaps, silent segments of student and impoverished groups? Before such phenomena can be explained, their existence and extent must be established.

EVIDENCE AND EXPLANATION

To illustrate the problems involved in evidence (establishing facts), consider the solved problem concerning the shape of the earth. Whether the world is elliptical ("round") depends on the type of evidence for the support of this "fact." Suppose you fixed a camera in one position and took a time-lapse picture of the stars over a four-hour period. If the sequence of pictures shows that any particular star has changed its position on a curved path, is this acceptable evidence for the elliptical shape of the world? If we started walking in a "straight line" from one fixed point and eventually returned to that same point (since it would take months or even years, students in this class should probably wait until the summer to try it), is this evidence for the world's shape? (This is not to imply that both of the authors can walk on water.; one definitely cannot, and this "fact" has not been established for the other.) If a spacecraft orbits the earth, is this evidence? And if pictures are taken during its flight showing the curvature of the earth, is this evidence? Is it evidence that ships eventually "go over the horizon" if headed directly out to sea? Contrarily, is taking a good look around you evidence for the earth being flat?

To put the two problems together, explanation and evidence, we know that salmon swim upstream and spawn, and it's almost always the same stream. How do we know this is an established fact? If it is a fact, how is it explained? Do salmon swim upstream because of instinct? Is this an explanation? Do salmon swim upstream because they experience physiological changes that make them require more oxygen (which they can get in fresh water) than at other times?

The above examples lead to two basic questions: When is a fact a fact? When is a fact explained or understood? Stated in terms of the subject matter of sociology, under what conditions have we established the existence of a structural characteristic, an act, or an interaction pattern? And under what conditions have we explained a structural characteristic, an act, or an interaction pattern?

These issues of evidence and explanation are characterized by some *dissensus* among sociologists. In fact, *dissensus* on these issues somewhat characterizes all the fields in the biological and social sciences. Diversity of thought ranges from the "hard line" notion that a fact is explained by subsuming it under a scientific law to the "soft line" notion that a fact is explained if we understand the reasons for its existence. Facts are explained, so some argue, if their purpose can be established, or if their composition can be described in detail, or if their simplistic nature or relations to other facts are discovered. With regard to evidence, although most scientists agree that it is based fundamentally on observation, there is some disagreement on observational techniques. One scientist, for example, may advocate only objectively verifiable techniques; another may accept subjective feelings between him and someone else; and still another may just know, because he is a member of the same group as the subject.

SCIENTIFIC ORIENTATIONS IN SOCIOLOGY

In sociology, there are three major scientific orientations; all three espouse a specific type of explanation, and two of them designate the nature of acceptable evidence. The orientations may be labeled functionalism, *Verstehen,* and positivism (which is sometimes referred to as logical positivism, neopositivism, or just the scientific method). These orientations and their conceptions of explanation and evidence are presented below. The section concludes comparing the three and relating them to the major substantive orientations in sociology.

Functionalism

In the social sciences functionalism has been used by many sociologists (and anthropologists) as a form of explanation of social and psychological phenomena for several decades. Emile Durkheim, mentioned under the structural orientation, was an early advocator of this approach as an explanation of social phenomena.[1] More recent sociologists following functionalism include such theorists as Talcott Parsons[2] and Robert K. Merton.[3]

The following assessment of the functional orientation may not typify each sociologist who labels himself a functionalist. Our attempt is to explicitly state those aspects in which there is a large degree of consensus and which delineate functionalism as a unique approach.

The functional orientation is characterized by six basic assumptions. The first assumption is that there is a system, social or otherwise, that is comprised of a number of inter-

[1] *The Rules of Sociological Method,* Sarah H. Solovay and John H. Mueller (translators), Glencoe, Illinois: The Free Press, 1938.

[2] *The Social System,* Glencoe, Illinois: Free Press, 1951.

[3] *Social Theory and Social Structure,* revised and enlarged edition, New York: Free Press, 1957.

related parts. A system can be an individual, a small group, a formal organization,'a society, or the world (among others).

The second assumption is that any system has certain basic needs that must be met, or the system will somehow die or change substantially. The human body needs oxygen and nutrition, and any society requires an institution for the care of children (a familial system) and a means to regulate behavior (a legal system).

The third assumption stipulates that to maintain a system in equilibrium, its parts must be meeting its needs. If the circulatory system is functioning improperly, the body becomes sick and imbalanced; and if the communication network is destroyed, a large scale organization cannot work.

Fourth, the parts of a system can be functional (contribute to the adjustment of the system), or dysfunctional (lessen the adjustment of the system) or nonfunctional (be irrelevant to the system). The rain dance may be functional for the Hopi Indians because it promotes group solidarity; suicide may be dysfunctional for Japan because it kills off productive members; and whether Canadian or American money is used in either of the two countries is at least, in part, irrelevant to what you can buy. Classifying these factors as functional, dysfunctional, or nonfunctional may be based on an explicit model of behavior or some vague and implicit notions on the social order.

The fifth assumption asserts that a need of a system can be met by a variety of alternatives or functional equivalents. The care of children can be handled by the immediate family or perhaps the state. Group solidarity may be fostered by consensus on a religious faith, or the threat of a common enemy.

According to the sixth assumption, only reoccurring activities or patterns are proper for analysis. A functionalist does not try to explain the functions or dysfunctions of World War II, but of all wars. He does not analyze how a particular family cares for its children, but how it is done by the family institution in a system.

The goal of functionalism, or a functional explanation, is to demonstrate the contribution or the maladaption of the parts of the system for the whole. A functionalist, for example, may attempt to show the necessity of the circulatory system in the human body, or the crucial nature of communication and transportation networks in complex societies. He may, however, attempt to demonstrate the negative aspects of war, crime, or discrimination for any particular human group.

In the social sciences two different types of functionalism can be delimited in conjunction with the substantive orientations. The first may be labeled structural functionalism and the second individual or psychological functionalism. The difference between the two is based on whether the system refers to a social group or to an individual.

A classic example of structural functionalism is the explanation of social stratification by Davis and Moore.[4] Social stratification, which is basically a prestige ranking of groups or individuals such as social classes or occupational levels, is functional for society, they argue, because it is the basis for filling society's essential positions with the most qualified persons. Stated otherwise, social inequality or stratification contributes to the normal functioning and serves positive functions for the state or society.

Davis and Moore imply that if all people were ranked and rewarded equally, society could not maintain its normal state. Society's important political, economic, and religious positions would either remain vacant or be filled by inadequately talented people. Either way, the society would be in a state of disequilibrium; it would meet its demise or change drastically.

Davis and Moore assume that there are only a limited number of people in society with the talent to adequately fill the important positions. They assume, further, that such talented people must initially sacrifice rewards so that they can be trained to fill the positions. The important positions, consequently, must have large enough rewards attached to them to induce such people to go through the training period. In

[4] Kingsley Davis and Wilbert E. Moore, "Some Principles of Stratification," *American Sociological Review, 10* (April, 1945), pp. 242–249.

short, the structure of society, in this instance the stratification system, is interpreted as contributing to the adequate functioning of society. It is functional for the system.

Another analysis that is frequently viewed as functional is Emile Durkheim's evolutionary ideas on changes in societies.[5] His study also has implications for the positivistic orientation presented later in the chapter. As a population increases in size, according to Durkheim, it exerts pressure on individuals to compete for its scarce goods. A given area has only a limited number of resources, and an increasing number of people must compete for them. Population pressure, consequently, increases the struggle for existence, which eventually reaches an acute level. To alleviate the struggle, the social division of labor (people specializing in different economic activities) increases, and societies change from a base of mechanical solidarity to organic solidarity.

Mechanical solidarity is characterized by (1) a low degree of division of labor (most people do the same thing, such as all the males being hunters or fishermen); (2) likeness and consensus among members, that is, they have the same beliefs, religion, and values; and (3) repressive or punitive law, that is, harsh criminal or penal codes. In contrast, organic solidarity is characterized by (1) a high degree of division of labor, such as in industrialized societies where there are many different kinds of interdependent occupations; (2) functional interdependence, for example, an automobile plant is dependent on steel mills for its raw material and its workers are dependent on agricultural workers for their food; and (3) restitutive law, that is, civil, procedural, administrative, and constitutional law.

Durkheim maintained that scientists should search for both the causes and the functions of social phenomena. In his study, population size and the struggle for existence may be viewed as causal factors. The increased division of labor and the change in the legal system may be seen as functional for society. The division of labor functions to re-

<hr>

[5] *The Division of Labor in Society,* George Simpson (translator), New York: Free Press, 1933.

duce the harsh nature of the struggle for existence; it allows people to become adept at one occupation and, thereby, increase productivity. The type of law functions to maintain the existing social order.

Repressive law, he argued, is necessary for societies characterized by mechanical solidarity, because a single deviant individual can upset its closely knit structure. If he challenges one person's beliefs, he challenges all. To maintain the society in harmony or equilibrium, the deviant must be harshly punished to bring him in line, or he must be eliminated altogether.

Restitutive law, in contrast, is functional in societies characterized by organic solidarity. In such societies, people are functionally interdependent; each person is dependent on others for essential goods and services. A deviant can upset the order of many others; for example, if one worker does not put the wheel on the car, the next worker cannot put on the bolts, and the workers who test-drive the car are left waiting. In this type of society, restitutive law is designed to quickly restore the order. Instead of eliminating the person, he should be made to do his tasks properly and keep the system moving. Restitutive law, therefore, restores society to its previous balance or equilibrium.

Some sociologists combine the structural functional and psychological functional orientations by analyzing the functions and dysfunctions for both society and the individual. Robert Bierstedt, for example, attempts to explain the universality of the family institution by specifying its functions for both units.[6] For society, the functions of the family are (1) replenishment of the species, (2) sexual control, (3) maintenance (providing the physical and economic support to maintain the child for society), (4) cultural transmission, and (5) status ascription. For the individual the functions are (1) life and survival, (2) sexual opportunity, (3) protection and support, (4) socialization, and (5) societal identification. Not only does the family, consequently, maintain the society in a

[6] *The Social Order,* third edition, New York: McGraw-Hill, 1970, pp. 394–403.

normal equilibrium state but it also is functional for the individual.

Religion is analyzed by Milton J. Yinger according to its functions for both society and the individual.[7] The universality of religion is "explained" by the fact that it functions as the ultimate source of social cohesion. The main values of a society are incorporated in its religious order. These values take on supernatural meanings in religion, which require that they be obeyed; violators are labeled sinful or evil. Religions bring the members of society together with regard to beliefs; that is, they promote social cohesion, and they are also a significant force in social control. Religion functions for the individual, according to Yinger, by explaining and justifying his suffering, frustration, hostility, and death—negative consequences of life that each person must face.

In each of the above examples, the part (stratification, the family, religion, or the division of labor) is explained in terms of its functions for maintaining the social or individual system. Although these parts of the system may seem essential for its adequate functioning, equivalent or alternative parts of the system may also meet the system's needs, and maintain the system in equilibrium. In a society with equal rewards for all occupations, for example, the important positions may be filled by mandates from a strong government instead of social inequality derived from an unequal distribution of rewards; sexual control of a population may be accomplished by a large police force rather than by the family; social cohesion may be promoted by mass communication or a uniform educational system rather than religion; and the struggle for existence may be alleviated by migration or death rather than by the division of labor.

Although the student may feel at this point that the functions or dysfunctions of phenomena are left to the scientist's imagination, a functionalist may use an explicit theory, his ingenuity, and years of learning before arriving at his conclusions. Rather flippant comments on functions are not

[7] *Religion, Society, and the Individual,* New York: MacMillan, 1957.

favorably received by the followers of this orientation. Very little is made of such comments as "the elbow functions positively for bar drinkers," "the function of prostitution is to keep women off the streets," or "the function of wisdom teeth is to keep bright dentists employed."

Verstehen

The method of *Verstehen*, which was advocated by Max Weber, has been used both as a technique for explanation and as an approach for establishing evidence.[8] It should be made clear that this orientation is seldom defended by sociologists as an explanatory technique in and of itself, and few sociologists are willing to say that it proves anything beyond a reasonable doubt. Many sociologists, however, use the method of *Verstehen* to some degree, and some claim it is the only technique for explaining social phenomena and gathering evidence. The trend in sociology, perhaps, is to accept both the scientific method with its emphasis on prediction and control and to try to subjectively understand human behavior. The method of *Verstehen,* it is argued, is the best technique leading to subjective understanding, which refers to empathy with the subject and the situation by the social investigator.

Followers of the method of *Verstehen* argue that social and physical phenomena are different. We can only predict and explain physical phenomena, some argue, but with social phenomena we can also understand. Understanding is possible because people make choices, have feelings, motives, personal values, and attitudes that are significant factors in their activities. Physical phenomena do not possess these human factors and, therefore, cannot be understood or studied by the method of *Verstehen.* Consequently, the traditional "scientific approach" of prediction and control is insufficient to "explain" human social behavior. We can also understand. The student should be able to see the compati-

---

[8] *The Theory of Social and Economic Organization,* Talcott Parsons (editor), A. M. Henderson and Talcott Parsons (translators), New York: Free Press, 1947, Chapter 2.

bility between social action theorists and those following the method of *Verstehen.*

This method may be considered as a personal "experience" in which a sociologist ruminates about an important problem for a period of time, and then, "in a flash," gets an insightful interpretation. However, as a form of explanation, *Verstehen* is based on the satisfaction a scientist has with his interpretation. This satisfaction may accrue from his imputation that the insight "makes sense"; for example, rape may be explained or understood as a response to sexual frustration, and suicides in concentration camps may be understood to arise from abject misery or hopelessness. The scientist, usually, must establish the motives of the actors or subjects before he feels he has a satisfactory explanation.

A recent example of using *Verstehen* as a form of explanation is reported in a conversation between Arthur L. Stinchcombe and Philip Selznick.[9] According to Stinchcombe, Selznick

"remarked that one felt satisfied that he understood something when he could summarize in a sentence the guts of a phenomenon. He gave the illustration that he felt satisfied when he realized that the achievement of the Bolshevik parties was "to turn a voluntary association into an administrative apparatus." To use, as a criterion of judgment, the guts of the phenomenon—what is going on—is better than to use any logical or formal criteria."

It is apparent that the guts of a phenomenon are quite similar to an emotional feeling or insight that makes sense. Another example of advocating *Verstehen* as a form of explanation is contained in the following statement:[10]

"As a simple and immediate test of the value of a psychological theory, I would suggest that you examine it and if it

---

[9] Arthur L. Stinchecomb, *Constructing Social Theories,* New York: Harcourt, Brace and World, 1968, p. v.

[10] D. Bannister, "Psychology as an Exercise in Paradox," *Bulletin of the British Psychological Society, 19,* 63, 1966, p. 26.

implies that man is much less than we know him to be or more significantly if it implies that you are much less than you know yourself to be, then such a framework should be discarded."

Verstehen as a technique for establishing facts or evidence is based on the ideas of *plausibility* and *estheticism.* Some sociologists may take exception to this usage of *Verstehen,* because the steps in the method are not clearly defined. Plausibility is based on three related factors. First, it refers to the acceptance of a statement or event as a fact if it seems reasonable, that is, it makes sense within the scientific framework. Second, plausibility is dependent upon the degree to which one has confidence in the ability of the observer. We may accept a statement as fact by an adult, but question it if stated by a child. Finally, plausibility may be based on the membership of the observer in the group he is studying. Many people, for example, are more willing to believe statements about blacks if they are made by a black person rather than by a white or Oriental. In its extreme form, this view may be summed up by the statement, "it takes one to know one." Evidence based on estheticism refers to the idea that the establishment of the fact is emotionally pleasing; that is, you have an emotional feeling that it is right.

A classic study that may be interpreted as using the method of *Verstehen* for both evidence and explanation is Howard S. Becker's investigation of marihuana or "pot" smokers.[11] Based on 50 unstructured interviews (a series of broad questions was asked), he maintains that he has explained why a person becomes a marihuana user for pleasure. Such an individual, he argues, must go through a process or sequence in which he acquires a conception of the meaning of the act and how others interpret it. Stated otherwise, the user must develop specific "meanings" or

[11] "Becoming a Marihuana User," *American Journal of Sociology, 59* (November, 1953), pp. 235–243.

"definitions of the situation" that are amenable to smoking marihuana.

These meanings are based on conceptions learned through a process that is conceptualized in three phases. First, the user must learn to smoke pot so that it can produce its effects. A person learns the proper smoking technique in a social situation with other users who teach him directly or are examples for his imitation. Second, the person must learn to recognize the effects of pot and connect such effects to the smoking activity. Quite often the novice must be told the effects, or told that what he is feeling is due to the marihuana. Stated differently, the user must be able to connect such responses as hunger, thirst, laughter, and being "high" to the act of smoking pot. In the third phase the user must learn to enjoy the effects he has attached to marihuana. Its effects, which include dizziness, thirst, and misjudgment of time and distance, must be interpreted as enjoyable. Crucial to the whole learning process are experienced users who continually define the situation for the novice by not only telling him what to expect but what to enjoy. Any person who has gone through the whole process, according to Becker, is a marihuana user.

From a positivistic point of view (see the following section), although Becker uses the interview technique, the unstructured nature of the interviews, the small number of respondents, and the lack of reliability of the data call into question the "facts" he claims to have established. On this rather loose basis, he claims that all persons who smoke marihuana for pleasure learn to enjoy these effects. The study has not been replicated and, perhaps, because of the vague nature of his methods it cannot be. Nevertheless, he accepts such characteristics as facts; his evidence, to a large extent, is based on the notions of plausibility and estheticism. Becker's explanation of the marihuana user is the learning process involved in the three phases. His explanation is, in general, based on subjectively understanding his subjects by ascertaining their motives, attitudes, and "definitions of the situation." He has not made a test of a designated hypothesis in terms of prediction and explanation; he has attempted to understand the behavior by an empathetic process.

Another example of using *Verstehen* for explanation and evidence is a participant observation study conducted by William Foote Whyte.[12] Briefly, in a participant observation study, the researcher usually stays with a particular small group or lives in a community; and while observing the members' behavior he participates in their activities to some extent. Whyte, for example, in his classic study of a street corner gang, took a room in the slum area, "hung out" with gang members, won the confidence of the leaders, and while participating in discussions and some activities he observed the behavior of gang members among themselves and with other gangs for three and a half years.

On the basis of his observations he came to a number of conclusions. To illustrate, he claims that (1) each group was characterized by a hierarchical structure that binds members to one another; (2) the groups or gangs were related to each other in a hierarchical way; (3) low status members could violate their obligations without changing position—in fact, their low positions reflected their past performance; (4) leaders were required to meet their obligations or they would endanger their positions; (5) each member was obligated to help other members whenever possible; (6) performance levels were related to one's position in the gang—for example, bowling scores were determined largely by the confidence members had in the player, and leaders usually bowled the highest scores; and (7) there was a high moral code with regard to sexual behavior—for example, those defined as "good" girls were not supposed to be touched, and those defined as "lays" were fair game.

Whyte's evidence and explanations were based largely on the method of *Verstehen.* His study has never been replicated; some of his findings have not been proved subsequently; and the reliability of his "facts" is questionable. Why, then, is his study considered to be important and acceptable by many sociologists? The answer to the question is not

---

[12] *Street Corner Society,* second edition, Chicago: University of Chicago Press, 1955.

straightforward, but the following three points are relevant (for all research of this type). First, he is trusted by his colleagues. They trust him to report what he saw, and not to ignore cases that may be negative to some of his initial findings. In short, many believe he is an objective observer of social phenomena. Second, he is considered to be a sensitive observer, in the sense of being able to detect the importance of social acts. By his excellent rapport with gang members, he could adequately probe beneath the surface responses to the "real" reasons. Finally, he has imaginative interpretations of his observations. Such interpretations have theoretical relevance, and apply to the results of studies in other areas of social phenomena.

Instead of his results being checked by others and then believed (the positivistic position), they are believed because of the faith others have in Whyte as an astute observer of social phenomena. With regard to the reliability of his facts, consider his observation that "good" girls should not be touched by the gang members. He gave the example that even when a "good" girl was drunk and asked for sexual relations, two gang members refused and took her home. To have a gang member refuse sexual relations with a very desirable and popular girl (that was how "good" girls were defined) is surprising—to have two gang members refuse is, perhaps, shocking. Yet a gang member informant told him about this incident, and Whyte accepted it as fact. Many sociologists have also accepted it as fact. Whyte did not observe the incident, but he trusted his informant, and it seemed plausible and esthetic. Even if the incident was true, does it mean that the gang members had a high moral code (an imaginative interpretation)? On the other hand, the two gang members might have been afraid of being caught, or were secret homosexuals, or wanted to hide the fact that they were virgins.

The final example of the method of *Verstehen* is a study by A. D. Fisher of Indian educational opportunities in Canada.[13] His major thesis is that the educational system is

[13] "White Rites Versus Indian Rights," *Transaction, 7* (November, 1969), pp. 29–34.

irrelevant to the Indians' desires and values. Stated otherwise, Indians are not learning in schools what is important to them in their everyday lives and for their career or occupational desires. They have been brought up to desire such occupations as ranching, farming, and auto mechanics, occupations selected on the basis of their knowledge and experience.

Besides teaching the English language and some rudiments of arithmetic and history, the major stress in school is on (1) dropping the Indian heritage, (2) teaching moral and ethical behavior, and (3) teaching prayer and patriotism. In this sense, Fisher argues, the school can best be defined as a rite of passage (a ritualistic activity); it is designed as a transition for the Indian into culturally recognized statuses and roles. Under the educational system, being a good Indian and being educated are not compatible. He feels that the incompatibility explains why Indians perform poorly in schools and have a high drop-out rate. Furthermore, because the school is incompatible with their desires, he claims that the educational system is failing the Indians; Indians are not failing the educational system. Fisher, moreover, believes that his thesis is relevant to the poor, black, and Indian in both the United States and Canada.

Fisher's explanatory thesis seems to make sense and is plausible and esthetic. Since it is not proved in any objective observational way, we can only accept his thesis on the basis of an emotional feeling. He does cite some evidence for his contentions, however. The fact that Indians perform rather poorly in school, for example, is based on the California Achievement Test scores among certain Indian groups.

It is somewhat debatable whether the participant observation studies by Becker, Whyte, and Fisher (often referred to as soft data investigations) should be considered under the rubric of *Verstehen*. The method of *Verstehen* does not include reliability (consistency of results from a given measurement instrument) or any clearly stated procedures. It is possible that two or more researchers could make similar participant observation studies with clearly stated procedures and derive similar results. Such investigations, which are fundamentally different from the single participant studies cited above, should not be placed in the *Verstehen* category, and actually are more readily subsumed under the positivistic orientation.

Besides using one as opposed to two or more observers and implicit as compared to explicit procedures, participant observation studies may be differentiated on the basis of whether they are used as a preliminary exploration that suggests certain facts and relations or whether they are used to establish facts and test hypotheses. Single participant observation studies that are exploratory probably should not be labeled as *Verstehen.* If used to establish facts and explain relations, however, they should be so labeled, because the major evidence is the emotional feelings of the researcher.

Positivism

Over a century ago, Auguste Comte advocated the positivistic position for the then new science of sociology. Comte argued that social phenomena are not basically different from physical phenomena and, therefore, the methods of the physical sciences could be used in the social sciences. Stated differently, by assuming that sociology, the study of social phenomena, is a science like any of the physical sciences, its body of techniques can therefore be subsumed under the general methods of science.[14]

Positivism, consequently, may be viewed as the use of the "scientific method" for the study of phenomena; it stresses clear procedures for acceptable evidence and an adequate explanation. A fact is explained, according to this orientation, if it can be subsumed under a scientific law, which contains a predictive statement that certain effects will occur given specified conditions. Scientific laws are statements of relations between two or more variables that have been supported or proved repeatedly by objective tests. The fact that you are able to sit (without being nailed to the floor) while reading this book is explained by subsuming the act of sitting

[14] George A. Lundberg, "Alleged Obstacles to Social Science," *Scientific Monthly, 70* (May, 1950), pp. 299–305.

under the law of gravity (which has been proved repeatedly, although few students are ever thrown in the air to see if they will, in fact, fall; if a few ascend further, the law of gravity would have to be modified at least to exclude such an unusual occurrence).

The primary goal of the positivistic orientation is to express the order (or the imputed order) in the universe in terms of scientific laws. One assumption, therefore, is that the universe, which is comprised of both social and physical phenomena, is orderable; that is, systematic relations exist between its elements. These relations, furthermore, can be observed and formulated into laws by scientists. The task for sociologists is to find the ordered relations among social phenomena and express them in scientific laws. Sociologists, depending on their substantive orientation, look for such order in the social characteristics of action, interaction, and structure.

Sociology is not at the comparatively advanced stage of trying to subsume laws under more general and inclusive propositions. The field can be more accurately described as in the stage of trying to gather evidence supporting some modest hypotheses. Hypotheses are testable statements of relations; that is, they can be proved or disproved by empirical test. If empirical, the variables in question are stated in such a way as to be subject to reliable observation.

At this rather modest stage of development as a scientific discipline, positivistically oriented sociologists are likely to emphasize the establishment of the causes of social phenomena by the scientific method. The establishment of causes is based on four widely accepted criteria: (1) association, (2) time priority, (3) nonspuriousness, and (4) rationale. Each of the criteria must be considered in conjunction before causality can be assessed.

An association is a necessary condition for the establishment of causation between phenomena. Social class must be related to delinquency before it can be considered its cause. If youths from lower, middle, and upper classes are equally likely to be delinquent, then social class cannot be the cause of delinquency. If athletic prowess is not related to ethnicity, then differences in ethnic origin cannot be the cause of such ability. Association refers to the notion that two variables or characteristics somehow change in conjunction with one another, or that they jointly occur with some regularity. To illustrate, occupational prestige is directly related to income (although not perfectly related for some low prestige occupations have a relatively high income and vice versa), and sex and delinquency are characterized by the fact that in an overwhelming number of countries most delinquents are males.

Time priority is another important criterion for establishing causation and refers to the idea that the independent causal variable must occur first or change prior to the dependent variable or the effect. Toilet training, for example, occurs prior to high school performance; child socialization occurs prior to adult participation in community organizations; and among females, physical maturation occurs prior to the ability to conceive. To return to a previous example, if social class is to be considered a causal factor in delinquency, it must not only be related, but it must also occur first or change prior to the occurrence of delinquent behavior.

A major problem in establishing causation is spuriousness, that is, the assumption that one event (or variable) causes another when they are only related. Suppose twin youths from Toronto received chemistry sets for their birthday in the summer of 1963. Suppose one unwrapped his present and placed a piece of the enclosed litmus paper in a blue solution, and in that instant there was an eclipse of the sun. He might have yelled to his twin, "Don't put the litmus paper in that blue stuff or you'll go blind." This interpretation is based on the erroneous conclusion of attributing the cause to two related events.

A nonspurious relation, in contrast, refers to a truly causal connection between two or more variables. A causal connection between two variables cannot be explained or accounted for by other variables. If the effects of all variables except those in question are eliminated and the relation between the causal variable and the effect is maintained, then the relation is nonspurious. If the relation between social class and delinquency, for example, is unaffected when computed separately for urban and rural residents, or for heavy, medium, and light teenagers, or for blacks, whites, and Orientals, then the relation is less likely to be false. This example assumes that urbanization, body build, and ethnic origin are the only relevant variables that could account for the relation between social class and delinquency. That is, if the effects of all relevant variables are eliminated and the original relation is maintained, then it is assumed to be a causal one. An example of a spurious relation would be demonstrated if ethnic origin predisposed certain persons to specific social classes, and also predisposed these persons to delinquency. In this illustration the original relation between social class and delinquency is explained by ethnic origin that occurred prior to both original variables.

The rationale, the fourth criterion in establishing causation, refers to the theory or interpretation of a relation stipulating that not only does the independent variable occur first but it also causes changes in the hypothesized effect or dependent variable. The rationale, consequently, is the justification for the observed relation, and may take the form of imputing an intervening mechanism that explains or interprets the relation. To illustrate, the hypothesized relation between social class and delinquency may be explained by the rationale that lower class youths lack the opportunities of those in the middle and upper classes, and to compensate for the lack of opportunities, they resort to illegitimate means to achieve success in society.

Evidence to a positivist is based on *reliability* and *verifiability.* Before any information is accepted as fact it must be observed repeatedly by two or more researchers; and they must come up with very close or similar results. If data are reliable they are supported by two or more observers, and if they are verifiable they are subject to more than one observation or test. A positivist, therefore, tries to clearly spell out each step in his study, so that it can be replicated by others. A replicated study is largely a repetition, but one or more aspects of the original study are usually slightly altered.

An example of positivistic evidence is the classic experiment in which litmus paper is used to discriminate between an alkali solution and an acid solution. The test has been replicated by different experimenters many times. If the litmus paper remains blue the solution is alkali; if it turns red it is acid. Although not based on such a simple experiment, if one wanted to establish the existence of racial strife in an area, two or more observers should be sent with detailed and specific instructions of what to look for that would clearly establish the existence or nonexistence (or extent) of such strife. Since this is seldom done, the positivist would stress that the single observer should clearly describe his procedures so others may replicate the study.

An experimental study in the positivistic tradition was conducted by Stanley Milgram on obedience.[15] Milgram's study (which has been replicated) has several implications for social phenomena. It suggests, for example, the powerful effect an authority figure can have on individual behavior. It also is indicative of the dominating effect of the social structure in determining individual behavior, regardless of individual motives and feelings. In other words, persons can be induced to behave in ways they feel are highly immoral. Specifically, he was attempting to answer the question, "Can a person be induced by an authority figure to increasingly punish an individual overtly protesting?" His experiment was based on personal conflict between the disposition not to harm others and the willingness to obey authority figures. His conclusion is that obedience dominates.

In a laboratory at Yale University using 40 male subjects from New Haven of diverse educational levels, occupations, and ages, Milgram carried out his experiment. It consisted of ordering each of the 40 subjects to administer increasingly severe shocks to another person in an adjacent room who was actually collaborating with the experimenter. The collaborator, consequently, was not receiving any of the shocks, but this was unknown to the subjects. The subjects were told by the experimenter (the authority figure) that the study was

---

[15] "Behavioral Study of Obedience," *Journal of Abnormal and Social Psychology, 67* (October, 1963), pp. 371–378.

designed to ascertain the effects of punishment on learning. Subjects were supposed to administer shocks to the individual whenever he gave a wrong answer, and to give increasingly severe shocks for each wrong answer. They were to start at the beginning low shock level of 15 volts and proceed up to a maximum of 450 volts. At 300 volts the collaborator in the adjacent room was instructed to pound on the wall; after the 300 volt level the collaborator made no more sounds and did not even answer the questions in the "learning" situation. The subjects were told that no answer is a wrong answer, and they should keep increasing the shock levels. If they hesitated they were prodded along by the experimenter with such statements as "please continue" or "it is absolutely essential that you continue." The whole situation was made quite "real" to the subjects; they believed that it was a learning experiment, that there was a victim receiving these mild to intense shocks, and that they were hurting him. The last shock of 450 volts was placed under a category marked XXX, which was more intense than the preceding category labeled "Danger: Severe Shock."

The results of the experiment are given in Table 2. Out of the 40 subjects, 26 reached the maximum shock level in the XXX category. Every subject proceeded at least up to the

Table 2.

Maximum Shock Levels Reached by 40 Subjects*

Shock Level and Voltage Range		Number of Subjects
Slight Shock	(15- 60)	0
Moderate Shock	(75-120)	0
Strong Shock	(135-180)	0
Very Strong Shock	(195-240)	0
Intense Shock	(255-300)	5
Extreme Intensity Shock	(315-360)	8
Danger: Severe Shock	(375-420)	1
XXX	(435-450)	26

* Adapted from Stanley Milgram, "Behavioral Study of Obedience," *Journal of Abnormal and Social Psychology,* 67 (October, 1963), p. 376.

intense shock level. That is, a surprisingly high level of obedience was found in this punishment oriented situation. Milgram maintains that his subjects did not enjoy giving out shock punishment; in fact, very common reactions by the subjects were extreme fidgeting, nervous laughter, sweating, trembles, groans, and stuttering. The subjects continued administering shocks despite these negative feelings.

Milgram's study is characterized by a precise formulation of the question, observable and reliable techniques for gathering data, and a large amount of control in the experimental setting. His procedures are explicitly stated so that others can replicate his study; consequently, it is an example of a scientific study in the positivistic sense.

Milgram's study confronts us with an ethical problem in social research. To what extent can human beings be used as guinea pigs in experiments? Obviously there are limits. We can hardly test the lethal effects of a new poison by giving it to human infants; and there would be a substantial reaction to a study that required adults to smoke five packs of cigarettes a day to determine the possible lethal effects of smoking. Milgram's investigation placed considerable psychological stress on his subjects and has been questioned on moral grounds. Perhaps a relevant question to ask about such studies is, what does humanity derive from their conclusions? If, for example, smoking five packs a day leads to a cure for lung cancer, more people may be receptive to the study (although there may still be a problem in soliciting volunteers).

The broader ethical problem in social research pertains to the extent social scientists can legitimately snoop into the lives of people and use up their time. One way out of the general problem is to give potential subjects the opportunity to decline, or to make questionnaire items optional. However, giving subjects a choice in taking part in a study may be more illusory than real. Some people have a difficult time saying no to a researcher. Perhaps the subject is of a lower status or is afraid of repercussions. As another problem in social research, although we may feel it is ethically necessary to explain the whole study to the subjects, such explanation may ruin the investigation. After learning that the study is on eating habits and weight, for example, the more obese subjects may not want to participate. Being ethical and carrying out adequate research, consequently, may conflict.

Another illustration of a positivistic study concerns parent-child relations and political rebellion carried out by Russell Middleton and Snell Putney.[16] In sharp contrast to the experiment by Milgram, this study is a general survey of 1440 students in 16 colleges and universities distributed throughout the major regions of the United States. As opposed to direct observational techniques and tests, the data are from questionnaires administered in 1961. A questionnaire is a set of related items or questions that are filled in or answered by the subject himself. (In an interview situation the subject responds to verbal questions that are recorded by the interviewer.)

Middleton and Putney's study has broad implications for the effects of the societal structure and its family institution on socialization of the young and rebellion among adolescents. Control of the child and the power of the society and of the parents are in question. The study is suggestive of the nature of the association between parent-child relations and adolescent rebellion. They hypothesize that adolescent political rebellion and estrangement from parents are directly related only if the parents are politically oriented and parental discipline is extreme (strict or permissive) as perceived by the child. This does not imply that all politically oriented and extreme disciplinary parents have politically rebellious adolescents, but only that a larger percentage of them do than nonpolitically oriented parents who are average in discipline.

Adolescent political rebellion is defined in terms of the different responses between adolescents and their parents in selecting one of the following positions: socialist, highly liberal, moderately liberal, moderately conservative, highly conservative, and no political view. Estrangement from par-

---

[16] "Political Expression of Adolescent Rebellion," *American Journal of Sociology, 67* (March, 1963), pp. 527–535.

ents was determined by the subjects' response to a question on how close he thought he was to each parent (very close, fairly close, not very close, and hostile). Finally, strictness of parental discipline was ascertained by the response to the question, "When you were in high school did your parents want to have quite a lot to say about your friends and the places you went and so on, or were you pretty much on your own?" ("Parents had a lot to say," "Parents had an average amount to say," and "Parents left me pretty much on my own.")

The results of the study lend support to the hypothesis that rebellion and estrangement are associated if the parents are politically oriented and discipline is extreme; for example, a strict parent advocating socialism is likely to have a conservatively oriented rebellious child. Parental indifference to politics and nonextreme disciplinary measures, consequently, may inhibit political rebellion among adolescents.

This study, by itself, is not sufficient to maintain that the relations in question are truly causal. Rebellion may occur prior to estrangement, and other factors such as formal education, peer group influence, or the mass media may precipitate political rebellion and estrangement, that is, account for the fact that the two are related. It is important, however, to establish the fact that there is a relation before its causal aspects are determined. The study, furthermore, has clearly spelled out procedures, and can be replicated by others.

Middleton and Putney's analysis has a direct bearing on multiple causation in the explanation of social phenomena. One aspect of their study is the attempt to account for the dependent variable of adolescent political rebellion by reference to the two independent variables—the extent of parental political orientation and the extremeness of parental discipline. Many scientists believe that all phenomena are caused not by one but by several factors. The use of multiple factors in theories, consequently, is considered essential for establishing causation and for predicting changes in, or occurrences of, events.

The last illustration of a positivistic study is a secondary analysis carried out by Gerhard E. Lenski on the effect of persons occupying inconsistent positions in society in terms of prestige and voting preferences.[17] A secondary analysis refers to the type of study in which a researcher uses the data gathered by someone else and usually for a different purpose. Lenski's study is based on an analysis of 25 national surveys of voting preferences, covering the period from 1943-1962, in four English-speaking nations in which Protestantism has been the historically dominant religion: Australia, Britain, Canada, and the United States.

He hypothesizes that persons occupying inconsistent statuses in a society are more likely to support liberal and socialist parties than those occupying consistent statuses. Status inconsistency refers to the fact that some persons occupy both high and low prestigious positions in society simultaneously. In this instance, the statuses of occupational class (divided into middle and working classes) and religion (Protestant and Catholic) are used to determine a person's inconsistency. The middle class is more prestigious than the working class, and in these countries, Protestants are historically more prestigious than Catholics. The hypothesis, therefore, may be restated as follows: middle class Catholics and working class Protestants are more likely to support liberal and socialist parties than middle class Protestants and working class Catholics.

According to Lenski, status inconsistency is a major source of individual stress, because people think of themselves with regard to their higher status, while others treat them in terms of their lower status. A middle class Catholic, to illustrate, thinks of himself as rather high in the status hierarchy (middle class), while others treat him as in a comparatively low prestige position (Catholic). This results in a conflict between personal expectations and experience, which leads to stress. A dominant response to this situation, he argues, is to react against the society by supporting political parties who advocate change.

The results of the study, in general, support the hypothesis

[17] "Status Inconsistency and the Vote: A Four Nation Test," *American Sociological Review, 32* (April, 1967), pp. 298–302.

relating status inconsistency to political preference. That is, those occupying inconsistent positions in the occupational and religious structure were more likely to prefer liberal and socialist parties than those in consistent positions. Out of the 25 surveys in the four countries, 21 were in the predicted direction. In Britain, however, there was only one correct prediction and two erroneous ones; this is a negative case for the thesis. Lenski suggests that the small Catholic population in Britain may account for the negative result, because it may mean that religion is not a salient or important status in the country. If it is not salient or important, there are no meaningfully perceived prestige differences between religions; and no matter what a person's religion may be, it would not be inconsistent with his occupational prestige. It should be noted that some recent studies on status inconsistency do not support Lenski's results. Although the theory is based on some provocative ideas, the consequences of status inconsistency are far from being proved or confirmed.[18]

Comparison of the Scientific Orientations

Functionalism, *Verstehen,* and positivism are the three major scientific orientations in sociology. They indicate the similarities and differences among sociologists with regard to what they will accept as an explanation and what they will accept as evidence. These orientations are not necessarily exclusive; one investigator may resort to any two or all three depending on the nature of his study, changes in personal preference, and his ideas about eclecticism in science. An eclectic may state that he not only understands your behavior, but he can predict and control it and, furthermore, he knows how it functions for society and the individual. He may claim not only to understand your aggressive response to frustration but also to be able to predict such responses for those under strict parental supervision, and to state its positive function for an individual in a competitive society.

[18] Leonard Broom and F. Lancaster Jones, "Status Consistency and Political Preference: the Australian Case," *American Sociological Review,* 35 (December, 1970), pp. 989–1001.

A sociologist, however, is likely to prefer one orientation over the other two. A positivist takes a "hard-line" or "hard-headed" point of view, which stresses explanation in the form of prediction and control of clearly measured phenomena. A functionalist emphasizes the establishment of the adaptive and maladaptive nature of characteristics, although he may also accept the positivistic orientation and try to establish the causes of events. He may, therefore, attempt to establish both the causes and functions of phenomena. Followers of the method of *Verstehen* are primarily oriented toward the understanding of events by determining the subjective states of individuals; they may also acknowledge the importance of prediction and control. They may, therefore, stress both the understanding and the explanation of social acts.

Those advocating any one of the orientations are likely to criticize the other two as somehow inadequate in accounting for social phenomena. A positivist may feel that the functional orientation (1) is incapable of prediction; (2) is vague in its definitions and use of concepts; (3) is unable to explain changes in systems; and (4) is basically tautological in nature —that is, no observational evidence is needed to support their statements. He may feel, furthermore, that the method of *Verstehen* is irrelevant to the study of social phenomena, because subjective states are not crucial to the explanation of human behavior, or if they are, they can be studied in a positivistic way. Those advocating functionalism or *Verstehen* may look unfavorably upon the positivistic orientation by claiming that it (1) overemphasizes observational techniques; (2) since social phenomena are different from physical phenomena, the methods of the physical sciences are not totally applicable to the study of human action; and (3) in their demands for measuring, positivists take quantification as an end in itself and, consequently, study the obvious. These criticisms and differences have not been resolved to the satisfaction of all sociologists, although some will adhere vehemently to their selected orientation. Sociology, consequently, seems destined to live with all three for some time to come.

SUBSTANTIVE AND SCIENTIFIC
ORIENTATIONS RELATED

There seems to be no logical reason for an advocator of one of the substantive orientations (structure, social action, interaction) to necessarily select a particular scientific orientation (positivism, functionalism, *Verstehen*), or vice versa. Some of the orientations, however, appear to complement each other to some extent, and there are definite patterns of choices among sociologists with regard to the two types of orientations.

Treated in terms of the substantive orientations, a structuralist, social action theorist, or an interactionist may all advocate the positivistic orientation at one time or another. That is, no matter what the subject matter, the social structure, individual motives, or behavior, the sociologist might choose a hard line approach to establishing evidence and explanation. Social action theorists, however, seem to be more frequent followers of the method of *Verstehen* (like Max Weber) than structuralists and interactionists. Both social action and *Verstehen* stress the study of subjective states, which is at least a partial link between the two. Structuralists, finally, seem to be either functionalists or positivists, or both. In fact, a structuralist using the method of *Verstehen* is a rarity, if one exists at all. The structural-functional orientation is a major one in sociology, and stresses the study of the functions and dysfunctions of structural components for the social system. A structural-functionalist may also attempt to predict and control social phenomena. From the viewpoint of the scientific orientations, a positivist may be a structuralist, a social action theorist, or an interactionist. Sociological functionalists, however, are dominantly structural in orientation, while followers of *Verstehen* are usually social action theorists.

The relations between the substantive and scientific orientations stated above do not exhaust all the logical possibilities. If you encounter a sociologist in either a research or teaching capacity, however, he is very likely to be a follower

Table 3.
Cross-Tabulations of Studies and Theories by Substantive and Scientific Orientations

Substantive Orientations	Scientific Orientations						
	FUNCTIONALISM		POSITIVISM		VERSTEHEN		Historical Evidence
	Explanation	Evidence	Explanation	Evidence	Explanation	Evidence	
STRUCTURAL	Davis & Moore's Stratification Theory		Marx' Capitalism				Davis & Moore Marx
	Durkheim's Division of Labor		Lenski's Status Inconsistency	Lenski			Durkheim
	Yinger's Functions of Religion		Blauner's Worker Alienation	Durkheim Blauner			Yinger
	Bierstedt's Functions of the Family		Strodtbeck's Jury Study	Strodtbeck			Bierstedt
SOCIAL ACTION			Miyamoto & Dornbusch's Self-image Study	Miyamoto & Dornbusch	Becker's Marihuana Study	Becker	
			Middleton & Putney's Adolescent Rebellion	Middleton & Putney	Fisher's Rights vs. Rites	Fisher	
				Weber's Protestant Ethic			Weber
BEHAVIORAL INTERACTION			Milgram's Obedience Study	Milgram			
			Simmel's Dyad-Triad and the Stranger				Simmel
			Bavelas' Communication Patterns	Bavelas			
			Homans' Exchange Theory	Homans			

of at least two of these orientations—one substantive and one scientific. Although the distinctions are useful devices for trying to comprehend a complex discipline like sociology, the student should be warned that it is not easy to label or classify all sociologists. The orientations, however, should help clarify the problems in defining sociology, in evaluating social research, and in giving an overview of the field.

An attempt is made in Table 3 to cross-tabulate by orientations all the studies and some of the theoretical works and theorists presented in Chapters One and Two. Each study, theory, or theorist, consequently, is placed in a row designating a substantive orientation (structural, social action, or behavioral interaction) and then placed in at least two columns, corresponding to the use of explanation and evidence in a particular scientific orientation (functional, positivist, or *Verstehen*). The table should help the student organize and integrate what has been said on the various orientations.

It proved to be a fairly difficult task to place some of the works and theorists in only one substantive and one scientific orientation. Placements were based, consequently, on what we perceived to be the scholar's most dominant orientations.

To illustrate the problem of classification, Durkheim may be labeled a functionalist, a positivist, or a follower of the *Verstehen* method, as well as a structuralist and a social action theorist. Each can be supported by the selective citation of a particular reference or book. His thoughts on religion seem to follow the social action orientation, while those on the division of labor in society and on suicide are more in line with structuralism. Our choice in placing him in the structural category is based on his early and rather clear statement of this position, and because of his heavy influence on many present day structuralists.

Simmel is a similar case. Some might argue that he made no substantive contribution at all; and that he is noted only for his informal observations of interaction, that is, his methodology. Others might say that he is clearly a social actionist in that his explanations were based on motivations and the social meanings of the situation to the actor. Others might even stress his structural thoughts concerning the effects of group size on interaction patterns. Classification, as with Durkheim, depends largely on which of his works are cited. If one were to ask for the real Durkheim or Simmel (or Weber, or Marx, among others) to please stand up, it is speculative as to whether one or several persons would stand, and if asked to stand at a later date, the "real" person may have changed.

Based on such problems, making your own decisions before viewing Table 3 should prove to be a useful learning exercise. You should then compare your classification to ours.

One immediate problem in placing studies or theoretical works in an evidence category is that some do not fit neatly into functionalism, positivism, or the method of *Verstehen*. We added, consequently, a fourth category of historical evidence. Evidence is considered historical if the scientist predominantly uses either secondary data sources such as census reports and vital statistics, or the personal accounts of historians, travelers, or other such writers. Historical evidence is supplied by others and may be based on the accounts of several observers (as in a census enumeration) or just one observer (as in a journalist's description of a battle).

History is frequently defined as the study of written records of past events. A major problem with such records is that they vary greatly in accuracy and detail. It is, furthermore, nearly impossible to determine their *degree* of accuracy.

Assessment of the utility of particular historical records depends to some extent on one's scientific orientation. For the positivist, the main problem with historical evidence is the reliability of the data. With this concern, it is important to know how the data were gathered; whether a standardized instrument was used such as an interview schedule or a questionnaire; and whether it was administered to a whole population or to a sample. The positivist depends more on data with these characteristics than on the impressionistic accounts of an observer, or on the descriptive accounts of a historian who has selected material from past records. If the data are based on direct observation of the event, then the positivist is concerned with the number of different observers and the consistency between them.

The position of followers of the *Verstehen* method is more favorably inclined to historical evidence. Such scientists are more concerned with whether (1) the information is supplied by someone they believe really understood the situation (because they were knowledgeable, or were there, or were members of the group studied), and (2) the observer is considered to be objective, intelligent, and giving plausible observations. Some functionalists, as well as followers of *Verstehen,* are more likely to use historical data based on the account of an event by one man or the interpretation of a historical period by a historian than is a positivist who restricts his use of historical data to more "reliable" documents.

The problems of reliable historical evidence are illustrated by reexamining Weber's study linking Protestantism to the rise of capitalism. Weber's thesis, simply stated, is that Protestant religious values (specifically those of Calvinism) led to the development of a capitalistic economic order. Some interpreters of Weber believe a more acceptable statement is that without the Protestant Ethic, modern capitalism would not have made its appearance.[19] The variety of interpretations of men like Weber and Marx attest to the problems of analyzing historical data.

One problem with Weber's analysis concerns the accuracy of his statements. Did the relationship, for example, between Protestantism and economic progress actually exist? Kurt Samuelson, examining Weber's data sources (among other sources) concludes that, "whether we start from the doctrines of Puritanism and capitalism or from the actual concept of a correlation between religion and economic action, we can find no support for Weber's theories. Almost all the evidence contradicts them."[20] It is unlikely that Samuelson

[19] Harry Elmer Barnes (editor), *An Introduction to the History of Sociology,* Chicago: University of Chicago Press, 1948, pp. 207–308.
[20] *Religion and Economic Action: A Critique of Max Weber,* New York: Harper and Row, 1961, p. 154.

has resolved the issue; he is criticizing Weber largely on the theorist's use of rather filmsy historical evidence. This evidence, consequently, neither supports nor refutes Weber's ideas.

SUMMARY

Basic to any science are the criteria for establishing evidence (when is a fact a fact?) and explanation (when is a fact explained or understood?). Sociology is characterized by some dissensus over the appropriate criteria on these two central issues. The dissensus revolves around the scientific orientations of functionalism, *Verstehen,* and positivism.

Briefly stated, the functional orientation is predicated on six assumptions: (1) a system of interrelated parts exist; (2) the needs of the system must be met, or it dies or changes; (3) the parts of a system must be meeting its needs to maintain a system in equilibrium; (4) the parts of a system can be functional, dysfunctional, or nonfunctional; (5) system needs can be met by a variety of alternatives or functional equivalents; and (6) analysis is appropriate only for reoccurring activities or patterns. The goal of functionalism is to demonstrate the contribution or the maladaptation of the parts of the system for the whole. There are actually two different types of functionalism: (1) structural functionalism, which focuses on the social group and (2) psychological functionalism, which focuses on the individual.

The method of *Verstehen* is based on the assumption that social and physical phenomena are different, and, therefore, require different techniques for study. Social phenomena can be understood as well as explained or predicted. Understanding comes from the satisfaction a scientist has with his interpretation of an event; the satisfaction may accrue from an insight that "makes sense." As a technique for establishing evidence or facts, *Verstehen* is based on plausibility and estheticism. Plausibility is based on acceptance of an event or statement as fact if (1) is seems reasonable; (2) one has confidence in the ability of the observer; and (3) the observer is a member of the group. Estheticism refers to accepting a statement or event as a fact if it is emotionally pleasing—a personal feeling that it is right.

The positivistic scientific orientation assumes that social and physical phenomena are not basically different. The techniques of the physical sciences, therefore, can be applied in the social sciences. Stated otherwise, positivism is the use of the scientific method for the study of phenomena. A fact is explained, according to this orientation, if it can be subsumed under a scientific law, which contains a predictive statement that certain effects will occur given specified conditions. The primary goal of the positivistic orientation is to express the order in the universe in terms of such scientific laws. At sociology's modest stage of development, positivistically oriented sociologists are likely to emphasize the establishment of causes of social phenomena on the basis of four criteria: (1) association of variables; (2) time priority of one variable as compared to another; (3) the nonspuriousness of a relation (that is, it is truly causal); and (4) an adequate theoretical rationale stipulating the reasons for expecting the relation. Evidence to a positivist is based on reliability and verifiability. If data are reliable they are supported by two or more observers, and if they are verifiable they are subject to more than one observation or test.

CHAPTER THREE

Evaluating Social Research

It is beyond the scope of this book and most introductory courses to treat the many important aspects of social research in depth.[1] Instead, this chapter is designed to aid the student in evaluating the adequacy of research studies by providing guidelines to judge the competence and scope of social inquiry.

Social inquiry requires a variety of decisions on several levels. Decision making, consequently, is an integral part of the research process. Students should try to understand why a researcher made one decision or choice and not another. Why, to illustrate, did he select a sample and not the whole population? Why did he select a general social survey and not an experiment? Why was participant observation used and not a questionnaire or direct interview? Why

[1] For a detailed account of how to carry out social research, see Sanford Labovitz and Robert Hagedorn, *Introduction to Social Research,* New York: McGraw-Hill, 1971.

was one measure of association selected over another? Several studies are presented to illustrate the nature and complexity of decision making in different kinds of social research.

The research process includes: (1) selection of the problem; (2) conceptual framework; (3) population and sampling; (4) research design; (5) observational techniques; and (6) data analysis. Selection of important social science problems and the conceptual framework are treated in general ways in Chapters One and Two. This chapter concentrates on evaluating sampling techniques, research designs, observational techniques, and methods for analyzing information or data.

EVALUATING THE SAMPLE AND THE POPULATION

Social research may be characterized by the study of a whole *population* (such as all persons in a country or business organization, or all delinquents or all females in a particular area) or the study of a *sample* of such populations. The population refers to the largest number of units or individuals of interest to the researcher. He wants to say something about the population by either describing its characteristics directly or inferring them from other knowledge. The sample is the part or segment that provides this knowledge and forms the basis for inferring characteristics about the population. Because of inadequate resources (small grants of monies, few interviewers, or limited means of transportation) or unavailability of the total population, sampling is often a necessary aspect of social research. To infer results to a population, the sample must be representative in the sense that it mirrors the theoretically important characteristics of the population. For example, if ten percent of the population has an income of $15,000 or more, so should the sample.

Criteria for Evaluating the Population

Sociologists almost always study human populations. It may not be always necessary, however, to study people to discover what governs their thought and behavior. A small number of sociologists (under the rubric of animal sociology) have been studying rats and other small animals with the hope of inferring their behavior to human populations. Rats, in crowded living quarters, for example, tend to develop ulcers, have a shorter than average life span, and rather poor eating habits. Perhaps these results apply only to rats and not to people in densely settled urban places as in ghettos or slums. Some of the results, however, seem to parallel human existence.

Whether human or nonhuman, there are four basic criteria that aid in evaluating the population in question: (1) precision, (2) completeness, (3) recentness, and (4) heterogeneity.

The *precision* to which a population is specified forms the basis for inferences from the sample. If the population, to illustrate, is comprised of the students at a particular college or university, decisions must be made on whether to include graduate students, part-time students, or enrolled students doing field work elsewhere. A precise population, therefore, is a well-defined one.

Some populations are conscientiously defined by researchers, while others are left implicit. In two studies by Pearlin and Kohn, the populations consist of the parents in Washington, D.C., 1956-1957 and in Turin, Italy, 1962-1963.[2] The authors did not have a list of every set of parents, and, therefore, their populations were somewhat imprecise; but, at least, they were specified in general terms. The parents were selected from lists of fifth grade pupils in selected schools.

Sometimes two or more social groups are combined to form one larger population for study. In an inquiry concerning formal organizations, for example, the authors defined their population as the personnel of a large nonprofit research organization, and the administrators and teachers of four grammar schools and one junior high school in a small town.[3] The research organization at the time of the study

[2] Leonard I. Pearlin and Melvin L. Kohn, "Social Class, Occupation, and Parental Values: A Cross-National Study," *American Sociological Review*, *31* (August, 1966), pp. 466-480.

[3] Robert Hagedorn and Sanford Labovitz, "Participation in Community Associations by Occupation: A Test of Three Theories," *American Sociological Review*, *33* (April, 1968), pp. 272–283.

had over 2000 workers, while the five schools consisted of about 70 members. The authors reasoned that the vast differences in purpose and size of the organizations would broaden the generality of the study. Every member of these organizations in the period of study (1965-1966) was treated as a member of the general population.

In a different kind of study by Molotch, the population was designated as South Shore, a community in the city of Chicago.[4] The physical boundaries of this community are only roughly specified, and the author does not say whether the results of his study apply to the whole community, to all communities of similar characteristics in large cities, or to any other designation. In contrast to these studies, in many experiments like the one carried out by Darley and Latané, the population is quite vague, and may not be specified at all.[5] The authors used students from introductory psychology courses at New York University. Do they wish to infer their results (described in a later section) to introductory psychology students, to all college students, to all youths (those under 30), to people in industrial nations, or to everyone in the universe? A clearer specification of the population would aid us in evaluating their research, and the extent to which their inferences may apply.

Recentness and *completeness* refer to population lists of the individuals or units involved. Often the best way to obtain a precise population is to actually list all units. The list can be evaluated on whether it has all the designated names and its currentness. Telephone books, for example, do not contain all individuals, because some people either do not have phones or have unlisted numbers. Furthermore, they are somewhat out-of-date even when issued. There is always a time lapse for any published material. The most current population lists are based on the recent past, not on the present. Since people move away, give birth, and die, it is

[4] Harvey Molotch, "Racial Integration in a Transition Community," *American Sociological Review, 34* (December, 1969), pp. 878–894.

[5] John M. Darley and Bibb Latané, "Bystander Intervention in Emergencies: Diffusion of Responsibility," *Journal of Personality and Social Psychology,* 1968, V. 8, No. 4, pp. 377–383.

very difficult to keep or obtain a recent and complete list. Most existing population lists, furthermore, like automobile registrations, Who's Who, and telephone directories, are biased against the inclusion of lower income people.

The final criterion for evaluating a population is *heterogeneity,* which refers to the difference among the units or individuals in question. Homogeneous populations can be represented by smaller samples than highly diverse ones. A larger sample is required from a racially and ethnically diverse neighborhood than from one characterized by a dominant trait. It takes a smaller sample to represent South Shore, Chicago (a relatively homogeneous lower income area) than Venice, California (which is more diverse racially, ethnically, and religiously). If people were completely alike in an area, it would take but one to represent all; and if all were completely different, no part or sample (no matter how large) would be representative. Although we can analyze the characteristics of bees from a very few, it would take a larger sample to represent the people of a small town (even if their population sizes are the same). Simply stated, people seem to be (given our current state of knowledge) more diverse than bees.

Criteria for Evaluating the Sample

Actually, there is one major overriding concern in evaluating a sample—how well does it reflect or mirror the important characteristics of the population under consideration? *Representativeness* is the degree to which a sample reflects the characteristics of a population. A lesser concern but of importance in some studies is the *adequacy* of a sample. An adequate sample is of sufficient size to permit confidence in making inferences to the population. Usually adequacy is a problem only in very small samples or when inferring to extremely heterogeneous populations. We would hardly have confidence in inferring attitudes on women's liberation from one female to all females in a country.

In most social research the representativeness of a sample is assumed rather than proved. Samples are often taken to determine characteristics of a population; consequently, the sample characteristics cannot be compared to unknown population characteristics.

Assessment of representativeness is hampered by limited knowledge and individual bias. If we possessed extensive knowledge of the population and if we displayed no personal bias in selecting units, then we could select those few individuals that represent the population. This is far from the case in social research. We do not know the "typical" few, and interviewers may show considerable bias when asked to select people in a community. Few are taken from ghettos or slum areas, and very wealthy areas are often underrepresented. Those individuals more often on the streets or in stores, and those available during the daytime (predominantly females) have a greater chance of entering the sample than most workers. Without some guidelines interviewers tend to select their samples in the most convenient way possible. Even if they are told to make sure that slum area residents are included, they usually will not go to the most dilapidated parts of the slums and they may try to select the more easily accessible people (again those on the streets).

Because of limited knowledge and personal bias, confidence in the degree of representativeness comes from the sampling technique. The most useful technique has proved to be some form of random sampling, because it helps control for the researcher's biases, and it provides a basis for the statistical manipulation of data. Such statistical manipulation permits the results of two different studies to be compared, and it precisely designates the nature of the inferential statements from characteristics of the sample to the population (see discussion of inference statistics, pp. 111–113).

A random procedure allows every individual in the population an equal chance to enter into the sample (even those in the most inaccessible areas). If the procedure is followed, then the researcher's biases are controlled within limits. The names of all people living in a particular area of a city could be placed on separate pieces of paper, placed in a large bowl, and thoroughly mixed. The researcher could then "blindly" select the individuals for his sample. An often used procedure is to give each name a number and then select the numbers by a random process. There are tables of "random" numbers that show no apparent ordering when reading off numbers from right to left, up and down, or diagonally.

The exact nature of a sample and the population it represents can be completely hidden in some inquiries. In the study of bystander intervention by Darley and Latané, the subjects consisted of 59 female and 13 male students in introductory psychology courses. These subjects constitute an "availability" sample (the researchers seized them because they were there and willing) and hardly represent any known population. We should be very cautious about inferring the results of the study to all humanity, to the people of the United States, to those in large cities, or just to those in New York, or even to students taking introductory psychology at New York University. The researchers did not use a random sampling procedure, and they may have a very biased (that is, unrepresentative) set of subjects. Are college students "typical" people? Are psychology students even "typical" college students? And are introductory psychology students "typical" psychology students? We simply do not know; a selection of subjects by a random technique would have helped. We are not trying to single out Darley and Latané for criticism; most experimental research does not use a random sampling procedure to obtain subjects.

Pearlin and Kohn, in their studies of parental values in Turin, Italy, 1962-1963 and Washington, D.C., 1956-1957, do use a random sampling procedure, but with a degree of complexity. They selected enough schools in each city to provide about an equal number of middle and working class parents of fifth-grade children. To accomplish this in Turin, they had to "oversample" schools with children from middle class families, that is, select a disproportionate number of them. The choice of families entering the sample from each school was made randomly from lists of fifth grade pupils. Their samples, consequently, do not represent the class distribution of either city, but they do reflect the characteristics of the selected schools in terms of middle and lower class families who have children in the fifth grade.

A *stratified random sampling* procedure may be used in place of the random technique described above. For a stratified sample the population is first divided into theoretically important categories (such as wealthy, middle income, and lower income strata; or males and females; or old, middle, and young age groups). Separate random samples are then taken of each category or stratum. This procedure ensures that an important variable will be sufficiently represented in the sample. For example, numerically small categories, perhaps an older age group or the extremely wealthy, can be "oversampled" to obtain a large percentage of these cases for analysis. We may want to select 75 to 100 percent of the extremely wealthy in a population but only 5 to 10 percent of other income groups.

In our organizational study,[6] a stratified random sample was taken from the "research organization." The personnel of the organization were stratified according to union membership and professional status. A 25 percent random sample was obtained from each of the following strata: (1) union members of skilled and semiskilled occupations, (2) nonunion members classified as technicians and technologists and acting as assistants to engineers and scientists, and (3) nonunion professionals, which included scientists, engineers, and management.

In summary, the evaluation of a research study requires that we determine the precision, completeness, recentness, and heterogeneity of the population. To judge the nature of the population, the reader should ascertain the degree to which it has been specifically defined; the date of the population list (if one was used); the inclusive nature of the list (whether it contains all persons in the defined population); and the diversity of the population (whether the persons are largely similar or dissimilar in social and demographic characteristics). To illustrate, compare a study of a large heterogeneous city that used a year old telephone directory that underrepresents the poor (without telephones) and the wealthy (with unlisted numbers) to a study using a population desig-

[6] See footnote 3.

nated by a week old list of all residents in a particular upper income white community. Clearly the latter study has a more useable and up-to-date definition of its population.

The sample, if one is used, should be representative and adequate. To evaluate these two criteria, the sampling technique and the size of the sample should be determined. To illustrate these points, a study of 2000 persons selected by a random process should be more representative than a study of 2000 persons haphazardly selected "off the streets" in a community. Further, a study of 2000 persons selected randomly should be more adequate than a study using only 20 randomly selected persons.

EVALUATING THE RESEARCH DESIGN

There are an enormous number of variations in social research: a small or large number of persons may be studied; the independent variable or stimulus may be varied in amount or strength, and may or may not be controlled by the experimenter; the study may take place in a small room, or in a large auditorium, or in several designated places, or in no particular predetermined place; subjects may be carefully chosen, or the selection may be based on a wide appeal to volunteers; subjects may be "forced" into a study (as in some prison camps), or persuaded by a monetary award, or an appeal to patriotism; a completely contrived situation or everyday natural surroundings may be used; the researcher may use precise and complex scientific measuring instruments or merely sit in a room and record his observations in a notebook; and the subjects may know they are being "observed" (as in an interview situation) or they may be relatively unaware of the observation (as in experiments using one-way mirrors).

The actual design of social research can be subsumed under three broad categories: the social survey, the experiment, and the case study. The many variations listed above can be applied to each of these broad types.

The social survey is characterized usually by a sample of a fairly large population and the use of a questionnaire or interview to gather information. Attitude polling techniques (such as those by Gallup and Roper in the United States) and the study by Pearlin and Kohn typify this research design.

The experimental design, in contrast, is generally much smaller in scope, and usually is carried out in some type of laboratory. The experimental variable or stimulus is usually carefully controlled by the researcher. Darley and Latané, for example, controlled the number of "bystanders" in their experiment.

The case study is an intensive investigation of one or a few social units (they may actually be individuals, families, a large scale organization, or a religious sect) and may involve an investigator living with a group while observing it. The study of South Side by Molotch illustrates the case study as does the work of an anthropologist who lives with a small nonliterate group for months or years. Jean L. Briggs, for example, not only lived with and studied a small group of Eskimos for a year and a half but was the "adopted" daughter of one of the households.[7]

A research design provides a basis for interpreting and assessing the results of a study. Poor designs permit conflicting interpretations; consequently, the effects of the experimental stimulus or the independent variable on the subjects are exceedingly difficult to determine, if they can be determined at all. If every time a subject smoked pot he also took LSD, we could not determine the independent effects of either one. If a riot broke out at the same time a Presidential speech was presented, we would have a difficult time ascertaining which one, if either, affected the attitudes of the population. If we wanted to know the effects of pot or the speech, then LSD and the riot are extraneous and confounding factors in the research. A good design controls for such factors and permits an adequate interpretation of the experimental variable, or it provides evidence for the validity of hypotheses.

One way of controlling for extraneous factors in an experi-

[7] "Kapluna Daughter: Living with Eskimos," *Transaction*, 7 (June, 1970), pp. 12–25.

ment is to use both an experimental and a control group. If two groups are treated exactly the same except that one group (experimental) is given the stimulus (special movie, therapy, drug, etc.) then the only reason the two groups can be different is due to the effect of the stimulus. Even an electrical power failure occurring during the experiment may not affect the results because both groups are influenced by the power failure. If the experimental group is different from the control group, and all other facts are controlled or are the same for both groups, then we usually can reasonably attribute the difference to the stimulus. There is still a problem, however, that the experimental variable and an unanticipated event like a power failure may interact in a complex way that ruins the experiment. Some of the subjects, to illustrate, who are positively influenced by a movie may feel the power failure is also part of the experiment and may react by becoming negative.

In an often used nonexperimental design called a *panel study,* controlling on extraneous factors can be more complex. The panel, which involves repeated observations of the same respondents over a given period of time, may use a special type of control group. The control is observed fewer times than are the members of the panel.

Subjects may become sensitive to filling out questionnaires or being interviewed every other week or every month. They may become, to the researcher at least, "different" people at the start than at the end of the study. They may learn or become sensitive to important factors of the study, or simply become bored with the whole research process. Repeatedly asking a person about an election campaign may induce an observable change in him. Such sensitization and change are serious shortcomings if we wish to infer the results of the sample to a population. The subjects may no longer represent the population from which they were sampled. To measure the occurrence or degree of sensitization of panel members, a sample control group may be interviewed only at the end of the study and their results compared to the panel group, or they may be interviewed at the beginning and at the end to see if its changes are more or less than the changes for the panel group. Consistent results between control and panel members indicate that sensitization probably is not extensive.

Whether a design is capable of providing an adequate interpretation depends on its evaluation in terms of four criteria: spatial control, temporal control, analysis of changes, and representativeness.

Spatial control is achieved by using both an experimental and control group in the design, and refers to the initial equality of both groups. This means that the experimental and control groups are highly similar on characteristics relevant to the study. For example, if the experimental group is composed of 25 female and 25 male freshman students with IQs over 120, then the control group should closely approximate these characteristics. If it does not, then any difference in the experimental and control groups after the stimulus is administered could be due to the different initial composition rather than to the effects of the stimulus. To cite an extreme example, if the experimental group was comprised of all geniuses and the control group of "dull normals" then it should not surprise us if after a speed reading course, the geniuses prove to be faster readers. This may well be the case even if the course had no effect. Consequently, equality in composition between the two groups is an important aspect for the interpretation of experimental results.

Temporal control, also achieved by the adequate use of a control group, refers to the elimination of the effects of extraneous factors over time. Suppose students overthrow the established power structure in a university while a small experiment is taking place on the attitudinal effects of a speech unfavorably disposed toward college administrators. The changing attitudes of subjects may be attributed to the student revolt rather than to the speech in the experimental situation. If a control group is used, however, the effects of the stimulus (the speech) may be separated from the effects of the revolt (which, in this case, is an extraneous factor). The factor of interaction, mentioned above, still may ruin the experiment.

Except for interaction effects, if both experimental and

control groups changed (and the control group did not hear the speech), then the student revolt could have been a major cause of the attitudinal changes. If, however, attitudes of the subjects in the experimental group changed and those in the control group did not (or changed less), then we can reasonably attribute the effects to the speech.

These conclusions are based on the logical setup of the experiment, in which the experimental and control groups are initially alike and are treated essentially the same except that the experimental group receives the stimulus. If the stimulus is the only factor distinguishing the two groups, any difference between them can logically be attributed to it. Without a control group, any changes in the experimental group could be due to a large number of extraneous factors as well as to the stimulus.

Both spatial and temporal control are achieved in the experiment by Darley and Latané by their use of subjects as witnesses with and without other witnesses or bystanders to an event. The authors created an "emergency" in their experiment by having the "victim" (in collaboration with the researchers) feign a nervous seizure similar to epilepsy while conversing with the subjects. Discussion sessions were held between the victim and a subject in three types of groups: (1) two-person groups (subject and victim only); (2) three-person groups (subject, victim, and one other, the bystander); and (3) six-person groups (subject, victim, and four others, all bystanders). The experimental variable or stimulus was the perceived number of others or bystanders in the situation.

The authors reasoned that as the perceived number of bystanders increased, subjects would take a longer time to report the "emergency" to the experimenter. This notion is in sharp contrast to the view that persons do not respond to real life emergencies (such as females being robbed or raped in large cities) because of indifference, apathy, alienation, or just not wanting to get involved. Rather than these reasons, it is hypothesized that persons do not get involved because there are other bystanders or witnesses to an event. If others are also watching a real life emergency, then no one is likely to respond for perhaps several reasons, such as (1) the expectation that others will respond, (2) the fear that a response in front of others could prove embarrassing, and (3) because any blame for nonresponse is diffused among all bystanders and therefore no one person is compelled to give aid or seek help.

The situation with no bystanders can be viewed as a control group in the experiment. The three- and six-person groups received the stimulus of one and four perceived bystanders, respectively. The authors did not attempt to maximize spatial control, because they did not equate subjects who went into the experimental and control groups. A degree of spatial control was achieved, however, because all subjects were of a similar age and education (freshman introductory psychology students). Temporal control also was achieved to some degree but was not maximized. Subjects were not run through the experiment at the same time and, therefore, different extraneous factors could have affected the results. The experiment, however, was carried out in a short period of time, which minimized the problem of separating the effects of extraneous factors from the stimulus. With these limitations in mind, the results of the study overwhelmingly supported the authors' hypothesis. Rather than apathy or alienation, the interrelation between bystanders (witnesses) appears to be an important factor in whether victims will receive aid.

If this result could be legitimately inferred to the United States, then the country may not be a "nation of sheep"— people dominantly self-oriented and afraid to get involved. "I'm for me first and foremost" would apply, if at all, to crowds, but not to single witnesses.

The third criterion for evaluating a research design is whether an *analysis of changes* of individual scores is possible. Change analysis can be made if subjects are measured or observed on some relevant characteristics in both pre- and post-test periods. Both experiments (if tested before and after the stimulus) and panel studies permit such an analysis. Subjects may fill out a questionnaire, take an examination, or complete a puzzle before hearing a speech or seeing a movie and again after such a stimulus has been administered. In the general survey design, change analysis is possible if the same subjects are measured on specified characteristics at two successive observation periods (that is, a panel study). Subjects could be interviewed twice in a three month interval, or their party preference could be determined in successive elections.

The major advantage of a change analysis is that the effect of the stimulus on each individual can be determined. Without such an analysis the overall group response must be used to analyze the effects. Suppose we wanted to determine the effects of learning nonsense syllables on IQ. We could compare the mean IQ scores between the experimental and control groups after the experimental group goes through the learning situation. We may find that IQ scores for the experimental group are substantially higher. In such a situation the assumption generally is made that all individuals in the experimental group increased their IQ scores uniformly. But this may be far from the case. Some subjects may have increased their scores by 10 to 20 points while others may have small increases or even slight decreases. By limiting the analysis to the overall mean IQ scores for each group, we would miss this differential response to the stimulus.

There are two disadvantages to obtaining observations on the same subjects twice and analyzing individual change scores. First, every time we observe subjects we run the risk of *sensitizing* them (that is, making them more aware of certain things) and changing their responses so that they are no longer representative of any meaningful group or population. If you measure the weights of a group of females and then go back a month later to do the same measurement, you are likely to get a reduction in weight whether the group was put on a diet or not. The second disadvantage concerns the notion of *regression effects.* Extreme scores (or just non-average scores) on many characteristics tend to be less extreme on subsequent observations. Because of imprecise measurement, for example, some persons with extremely high IQ scores in an initial observation period tend to have slightly lower IQ scores in a subsequent period. Children of very tall parents tend to be slightly shorter, on the average, than their parents. Everything else must be equal, of course, like a similar diet for both parents and children in the early periods of their lives. The point is that certain persons may definitely change on a characteristic, but it is due to the regression effect rather than to the stimulus. Researchers should be very careful not to attribute the cause of such changes to the stimulus or independent variable.

The final criterion for evaluating a research design is *representativeness,* which not only refers to sampling as stated previously but also to the utilization of realistic situations. Do subjects in a laboratory experiment behave differently than they would in their home environment? Perhaps some persons withdraw in experimental situations, although they are quite open and loquacious in familiar settings. A speed reading course may change their behavior in the laboratory but not at school. Would the subjects in the experiment by Darley and Latané respond the same if their discussion took place with a stranger on the street who was actually experiencing an epileptic seizure? Experimental studies can be very beneficial to the establishment of causation, but if the setup is too contrived or unrealistic, it is difficult to infer the results to more "normal" settings.

In summary, research designs can be evaluated on four criteria: (1) spatial control, (2) temporal control, (3) analysis of changes, and (4) representativeness. Experimental designs are often set up to maximize spatial and temporal control, and may permit change analysis if observations are made at two separate periods. Experiments, however, are often nonrepresentative because they are not based on random samples and they may take place in highly contrived situations. In contrast, surveys often are based on rather large random samples, and persons are observed or interviewed in their natural surroundings (home or work). Few surveys, however (except for the panel study) use a control group and most use only one observation period. Consequently, surveys often lack spatial and temporal control and do not permit a change analysis. The survey by Pearlin and Kohn on the values of parents in Washington, D.C. and Turin, Italy follows this description rather closely. Compared to the experiment and the survey, the case study (such as the one by Molotch of South Shore) tends to be weak on all four criteria. Case studies do not use a control group; there is generally one rather long observation period, and sampling is not involved. Most, however, take place in a natural setting, and they may suggest hypotheses that can be studied in a more rigorous manner.

EVALUATING OBSERVATIONAL TECHNIQUES

There is a wide variety of techniques for observing social phenomena. Most social surveys are based on a questionnaire (subjects fill out the questions themselves) or interview (subjects are asked the questions by an interviewer who fills in their answers). Some surveys and case studies may also use persons who directly observe social situations. Such observers may participate in a community and record their observations in a notebook or daily log. Whyte's study of a street corner gang typifies such participant observation (Chapter 1).[8] Surveys, case studies, and especially experiments may use mechanical devices or a combination of observational techniques. Mechanical devices include tape recorders, cameras, and interaction chronograph machines (a device used to record the initiation and length of communications). In any design the somewhat indirect techniques of physical trace evidence may be employed. Such evidence is based on what persons or groups build up and leave behind or partially use. To illustrate, the pottery remains and burial deposits of nonliterate groups indicate the complexity of life style, and wear on steps, books, and shoes indicate the extent to which each is used.

Two basic criteria may be used to evaluate observational techniques: *reliability* and *validity.* A technique is reliable if repeated observations of the same phenomenon with the same instrument yield similar results (except for an actual

[8] William Foote Whyte, *Street Corner Society,* Chicago: The University of Chicago Press, 1943.

change from one observational period to the next). A valid technique measures what the researcher wants it to measure; that is, it reflects its theoretically defined dimension.

To illustrate both criteria, an IQ test is reliable if an individual achieves the same score two or more times, and it is valid if it measures the theoretical meaning stipulated by the researcher. The theoretical meaning may pertain to innate intelligence or to achievement in the American middle class educational system. There is ample evidence that IQ tests do not measure innate intelligence (at least not exclusively); it is, therefore, an invalid observational technique if used for this purpose. It should be evident that if a technique is not reliable, it cannot be valid. That is, it cannot be measuring what you want it to if it yields different results at different applications (except for an actual change). A measure, however, can be reliable but invalid. IQ tests may yield the same scores for a group of individuals; but the test may not reflect the researcher's theoretical meaning.

Reliable measures require clearly designated procedures so that different observers, or one observer in two different time periods, may interpret the measure in the same way. If observers disagree or change the observational technique over time, then it is unreliable. Clearly designated procedures require *operational definitions*, which specify what competent observers must do in order to come up with the same results when measuring the same thing. Examples of operational and reliable measures are height measured by a ruler, temperature measured by a thermometer, length of interaction measured by a watch, and, perhaps, marital happiness measured by the response to the question, "Are you happily married? Yes___, No___" (could this measure be reliable but invalid?).

A basic problem in establishing the reliability of an observational technique concerns the interplay between a memory factor and a time-related change factor. Persons who retake IQ tests generally achieve a higher score the second time (except for extreme scores), because they have learned how to take the test and have memorized certain types of questions. This memory factor, by producing different scores, is detrimental to reliability. To reduce the effect of memory on reliability the test-retest interval may be lengthened, so that a subject may forget some important factors he picked up initially. The longer the interval, however, the greater the probability that the subject has actually changed. An increase in score, consequently, may be due to an actual (valid) change in the person rather than a memory factor. Ideally, the test-retest should take place at the same time to eliminate the time and memory factors. Since this is impossible, unreliability is a problem in all social research. In evaluating the reliability of observational techniques, therefore, potential memory factors and the time interval between tests should be considered along with the degree of similarity of scores in both periods.

One research strategy designed to overcome both the time and memory factors is *split-half reliability.* If test questions or questionnaire items are theoretically assumed to be measuring similar phenomena, then the first half or the odd numbered items may be correlated with the second half or even numbered items. A high correlation indicates that the test or questionnaire is reliable.

Validity also is a vexing problem in social research. Actually measuring what you want to measure requires some operational standard for comparison. To make sure that you really have a foot ruler (that is, that you have a valid measure of one foot), you could compare it to an agreed upon standard foot ruler. If they are of the same length, then you have established the validity of your measure (in terms of the standard measure). However, as characterizes almost all observational techniques in social research, standard measures do not exist. It is useless to compare two different techniques if there is no reason to believe that either measure is valid.

Without a standard, the degree of validity of any technique may be approximated only by indirect methods. Two of the most prominent indirect methods for establishing validity are (1) prediction of an outside criterion and (2) theoretically meaningful results.

Suppose on the basis of marital happiness, divorce and

personal stress can be predicted to a substantial degree. Individuals who are happily married (by responding yes to the question, "Are you happily married?") are less likely to get a divorce and experience stress than those giving an unhappily married response. The predictive nature lends confidence to the validity of the technique. It does not, however, establish validity in any absolute sense. The question may seem to tap marital unhappiness, but really may reflect religious beliefs or the extent of one's religious background. Deeply religious persons, for example, may feel they must respond that they are happily married no matter what kind of married life they have. Religious beliefs, rather than marital happiness, may be predictive of divorce and personal stress. Predictive ability, consequently, only lends support to the validity of a technique; it does not prove it.

The second indirect method, often called face validity, refers to theoretically meaningful results. For example, suppose we devised a measure of national planning among countries. If the derived values of national planning "make sense" according to a theory or model, then the validity of the technique is supported (but again not proved).

The reliability and validity of the observational techniques mentioned previously (such as questionnaires, interviews, human observers, mechanical devices, and physical trace evidence) may now be assessed. Precisely worded questionnaires and interviews, for example, tend to be more reliable than those using broad questions. Reliability tends to be higher for the marital happiness question discussed above than for one asking vaguely, "How is your married life?" Participant observation generally is a less reliable technique than are questionnaires and mechanical devices. Often the guidelines for observing are few and vague so that two or more observers are not likely to come up with similar results. Would another observer besides Molotch arrive at the same conclusions in his study of South Shore? Mechanical devices, like a camera or scale, are usually quite reliable, while the reliability of physical trace evidence often is difficult to determine.

The reliability and validity of the questionnaire and interview are affected by several factors. Asking questions may sensitize persons so that they respond differently than if they were not asked. Sensitization, as in the case of asking a group of females their weight, can destroy the validity of an observational technique. Furthermore, subjects' memories are often spotty or faulty or the subject may lie. All of these factors can adversely affect both reliability and validity.

Most observational techniques have some bias and are, therefore, unreliable or invalid to some extent. The biases of the different techniques, however, often do not overlap. Consequently, an excellent technique to control for unreliability and invalidity is to use two or more observational techniques in a study. If the different techniques (possessing somewhat different biases) come up with similar results, then the reliability and validity of the results are supported (but again not proved). To illustrate, a person may (1) respond to a question that he is happily married and (2) be observed directly to have few arguments and to spend a great deal of time with his wife. It could be that he responded he was happily married because of religious beliefs (as stated previously); and he seldom argues with his wife because he seldom talks to her at all; and he spends a great deal of time with her because he does not have anything else to do. But all three of these results simultaneously are less likely than any one of them alone. Therefore, the consistent observations that he is happily married are supportive and lend a degree of reliability and validity to the classification.

Depending on their substantive and scientific orientations, validity and reliability receive differential emphasis by social researchers.[9] Positivists, with their concern for operational definitions, appear to stress the reliability of measures of behavior or attitudes first; if reliability is achieved, then the

[9] For an interesting exchange on this topic and its ramifications for predicting behavior from attitudes, see Irwin Deutscher, "Looking Backward: Case Studies on the Progress of Methodology in Sociological Research," *American Sociologist, 4* (February, 1969), pp. 35–41; Richard T. LaPierre, "Comment on Irwin Deutscher's Looking Backward," *American Sociologist, 4* (February, 1969), pp. 41–42; Icek Ajzen, *et al.,* "Looking Backward Revisited: A Reply to Deutscher," *American Sociologist, 5* (August, 1970), pp. 273–276.

problem of validity can be assessed. This emphasis is based on the notion that reliability is a necessary condition for validity—if a measure is not reliable, validity cannot be assessed.

The positivistic orientation has been criticized on the grounds that it loses sight of validity (measuring the truth or the theoretical meaning), and that it ritualistically belabors replication of studies and the repeated use of measuring instruments (like questionnaires, interview schedules, and paper and pencil tests). Even if reliability is achieved, without validity, so the argument goes, we do not know what we have, and we are as much in the dark as ever about understanding social behavior. Although reliable measures may be predictive of behavior or motives, we cannot establish knowledge if we do not know the true meanings of the measures. Prediction can be achieved, consequently, without ever knowing why or how. In the extreme, prediction is viewed as essentially meaningless, because it is based on simplistic and unreal ideas of cause and effect. (A positivist may retort that without some degree of predictability, there can be no understanding.)

Likely advocators of this view are those following the orientation of *Verstehen,* which includes several action theorists, symbolic interactionists, and some radical and black sociologists. These scientists are likely to emphasize validity first; and if achieved, then perhaps concentrate on the problem of reliability of measurements. Validity, which is measuring what the researcher wants to measure or tapping the essence or truth, is viewed as the crucial problem.

The validity problem is minimized according to this view, if direct observation of behavior is used rather than the use of measuring instruments (usually the questionnaire or interview). Presumably, direct observation is what we approximate with our measuring instruments.

Those advocating direct observation (and emphasizing validity over reliability) are likely to favor participant observation studies and direct contact with subjects. Positivists (emphasizing reliability over validity) are likely to favor studies employing measuring instruments used as a basis for operational definitions.

In summary, if establishing validity is viewed as the major problem, then participant observation studies based on direct observation of behavior are frequently advocated. These studies are characteristic of followers of the *Verstehen* scientific orientation (which includes many action theorists, symbolic interactionists, and some radical and black sociologists). If, however, reliability is viewed as the major problem, then perfecting and using measuring instruments are advocated and may be employed in any type of survey, experiment, or case study. The use of measuring instruments is characteristic of the followers of the positivistic orientation (which may include some structuralists, social action theorists, and behavioral interactionists).

It should be stressed that most scientists (whether followers of the positivistic or *Verstehen* orientations) do not totally disregard reliability or validity, but only that one is emphasized over the other. This emphasis, however, leads to very different kinds of empirical inquiries—direct observation as opposed to using measuring instruments. It is usually assumed by the followers of *Verstehen,* furthermore, that direct observation is the only way to establish underlying motives—measuring instruments do not accurately tap this dimension.

In summary, there are two basic criteria for evaluating observational techniques: reliability and validity. A reliable technique yields similar results in repeated observations of the same phenomenon. A valid technique measures a theoretically defined dimension—it measures what it is supposed to measure. In sociology, the degree of validity of an observational technique (like direct observations, interviews, and mechanical devices) only can be estimated, because of a lack of a standard measure or criterion of important variables. Two prominent indirect methods for establishing validity are predicting an outside criterion and obtaining theoretically meaningful results.

EVALUATING DATA ANALYSIS

After gathering information, the researcher, guided by the nature of the problem and the theoretical formulation, is in a position for analysis and interpretation. Analyzing and interpreting are essential procedures, because information must be given meaning before it is useful.

The information from most social research is incomprehensible in its raw form. To have the income and educational levels of 1500 persons provides an overwhelming number of different bits of data. Few if any researchers can handle the number of dollars and cents earned per year for all these persons, let alone be able to juggle in their minds their exact educational levels, age, sex, marital status, memberships in community organizations, attitudes toward contemporary society, personal values, and occupations. Even if they could, it would be nearly impossible to communicate these results to others in their entirety, which would hinder the distribution of knowledge and the replication of studies. Communicating results and replication are necessary procedures for the development of science.

To make a large amount of information comprehensible, it must be "reduced" to a small number of meaningful values that are closely tied to the following: (1) theoretical formulation, (2) operational interpretability, and (3) communicability. These three criteria are useful aids in evaluating data analysis procedures, which usually include statistical techniques.

Theoretical Formulation

The statistical manipulation of data must be closely tied to the theoretical formulation for meaningful data reduction. There would be no scientific reason to measure the social class composition of a society unless it was considered to be an important characteristic distinguishing one society from another or determining the behavior and life style of its members. The proportion of persons in a society with a per capita income above $30,000 is an isolated and meaningless fact unless tied to such characteristics as the differential power or ability to make decisions, control over those with lower per capita income, disproportionate numbers in professional and managerial occupations, and a style of life that includes a distinctive set of behaviors, values, social norms, attitudes, and interaction patterns. Stated otherwise, a particular set of data or any fact is meaningless unless theoretically tied to other phenomena—in isolation, it is useless to the development of a science.

The participant-observation study by Harvey Molotch ties a series of observations on the behavior and interaction between blacks and whites to a rather loosely stated theoretical formulation on racial discrimination and prejudice. Molotch maintains that intimate personal relations between persons in cities are limited by the large number of people and daily contacts. Each person, consequently, must be highly selective in his friendship choices. Because of the large number of people and their suspicious and untrusting feelings of others who are unknown or strange, certain cues are used to avoid "enemies," determine possible "friends," and predict the "intentions" of others. These cues are either tied to some kind of interpersonal similarity between persons, or they are based on personal ties among friends or familial relationships. Such similarities or ties are assumed to imply dependability and trustworthiness between the interacting parties. Without these cues mutual avoidance or hostility results between persons or groups. Consistent with this formulation, settings requiring intimate relations will be characterized by a high degree of segregation.

(Could it be on the basis of this formulation that men are more likely to have intimate contacts with other men than with women, because men are more similar to men and, therefore, more trustworthy of one another? The same applies to intimate contacts between women, of course. Could this formulation explain homosexuality to some extent? For the sake of the survival of mankind, it seems best if Molotch's formulation applies more to race and ethnic origin, rather than to sex.)

Molotch applies this theoretical formulation to his study of racial relations in South Shore, Chicago. He maintains there are many differences between whites and blacks that minimize their similarities and personal ties and lead to mutual avoidance and, at times, even to open hostility. To illustrate, blacks and whites have different religious, family, and leisure patterns, they often dress differently, they sound different, and young blacks even walk differently. These differential characteristics lead to mistrust and to feelings that the opposing group is not dependable.

Consistent with this formulation, Molotch studied three forms of racial integration: (1) *demographic,* that is, a specified area is characterized by the presence of both blacks and whites; (2) *biracial interaction,* exemplified by nonantagonistic black-white interrelations; and (3) *transracial solidarity,* which refers to free, unrestrained biracial interaction, where race is not an important factor in friendship. He tried to assess the degree to which each of the three forms of racial integration occurred in South Shore by studying interaction in retail stores, social settings, outdoor recreation, schools, religious institutions, and voluntary associations.

Although the South Shore area is characterized by demographic integration (it is about one third black), Molotch found few instances of biracial interaction or transracial solidarity. These observations are consistent with the theoretical formulation anticipating mutual mistrust and avoidance between blacks and whites, because of dissimilarities in appearance, life style, and lack of personal ties.

Several observations illustrate the accuracy of the prediction that blacks and whites avoid one another, and especially in situations requiring intimacy. Although both groups, for example, will shop in the same retail stores, those stores rendering personal services and based on some degree of intimacy (like barber and beauty shops) were almost totally segregated. Segregation in social and recreational settings, furthermore, increased on Saturday night. Saturday night activities, such as in bars and bowling alleys, are based on a greater degree of intimacy than at other times, which leads to the prediction of less integration. Consistent with this observation, social activities become more segregated at night than in daytime hours. Outdoor recreation facilities, like beaches and parks, also were characterized by segregation, as were most of the public schools in South Shore.

Table 4 shows the segregation patterns in religious institutions. Social activities connected with church life were almost completely segregated and confined to whites. The

Table 4.

Racial Composition of South Shore's Christian Churches and Church-Related Schools

Denomination of Church	Church Members (parishioners)	Blacks Membership	% Black	Sunday Attenders	Black Sunday Attenders	% Black	Enrolled in Sunday School	Black in Sunday School	% Black
PROTESTANT:									
Community	1775	14	.8	625	27	4.3	350	160	45.0
Episcopal	450	30	6.6	250	25	10.0	87	20	23.0
Lutheran	305	25	8.0	113	10	8.8	45	25	55.0
Methodist	650	25	3.8	200	30	15.0	390	250	64.0
Methodist	210	21	10.0	90	9	10.0	159	157	99.0
Christian Science	250	1	.4	250	7	2.8	160	12	7.5
Bible Church	75	5	6.6	65	35	53.0	150	100	66.0
Subtotals	3715	121	3.3	1593	143	8.9	1360	724	53.0
Nine Other Protestant Churches	2285	0	...	994	0	...	140	0	...
Protestant Totals	6000	121	2.0	2587	143	5.5	1500	724	48.0
CATHOLIC:[a]									
1) Catholic	1200[b]	70[b]	5.0	4000	100	2.5	485	110	23.0
2) Catholic	1900[b]	1[b]	.5	3000	0	...	200	10	5.0
3) Catholic	2700[b]	325[b]	12.0	9000	477	53.0	732	40	5.5
Catholic Totals	5800[b]	396[b]	6.8	16000	577	3.6	1417	160	11.0

[a] Catholic school data refer to day school enrollments, not Sunday school. Except for Church No. 3, attendance data based on actual head counts on a Sunday, Spring, 1966.

[b] Refers to number of families, rather than individuals.

Other sources: Reports of clergymen.

Adapted from Harvey Molotch, "Racial Integration in a Transition Community," American Sociological Review, 34 (December, 1969), p. 887.

percentage of blacks who attend church services on Sunday was usually greater than the percentage of black members; and the percentage of blacks attending Sunday school (mostly children) is far in excess of the percentage who are members. These observations are consistent with the theoretical formulation that contacts or settings requiring intimacy are characterized by a higher degree of segregation.

The information contained in Table 4 and the observations by Molotch are meaningful in terms of the theoretical formulation. The observation that blacks and whites are seldom integrated in a biracial interaction or transracial solidarity sense is sociologically meaningless until it is tied to some type of theoretical reasoning. In this case, Molotch has attempted to explain and predict the segregation practices between blacks and whites.

The major exception to the avoidance patterns occurred in the biracial membership and leadership of an organization called South Shore Commission. The transracial solidarity in this group was based on a shared and deviant ideology, biracial equality in status and organizational usefulness, and few previous organizational ties.

Like the investigation by Molotch, the study by Pearlin and Kohn also illustrates meaningful data reduction by closely tying information to a theoretical formulation. They contend that occupation or work is a salient position in one's life and influences individual values. Occupational groups furthermore characterize broad social classes. Middle-class occupations require a greater degree of self-direction than working-class occupations, which require more obedience.

The authors assume that what parents value for their children are the characteristics important to the circumstances of the parents' lives. Pearlin and Kohn reason, consequently, that middle-class parents will value self-direction and self-control for their children more highly than will working class parents. Parents from the working class will place a greater value on conformity to external proscription, which results in obedience. Briefly stated, the middle class is characterized by self-control while the working class is characterized by obedience. These values largely result from the different requirements of middle and working class occupations, which are characterized by self-direction and following orders, respectively.

Although Pearlin and Kohn found cultural differences between Italian and American parents (American parental values are more child-centered, for example), the relation between social class and parental values was essentially the same in both countries. Some of the cultural and occupational comparisons are presented in Table 5. Consistent with their theoretical orientation, middle-class parents predominantly emphasized self-control while working class parents predominantly emphasized obedience. However, despite the agreement between parents of both countries in giving the highest priority to honesty as a value for their children, American parents are more likely to value happiness, popularity, and consideration, while Italian parents are more likely to value manners, obedience, and seriousness. Italian working class values, furthermore, are even more "conservative" than American working class values. Although there are differences between the two countries, the overall results support the thesis that middle-class parental values emphasize self-direction (self-control), while working-class parental values emphasize conformity to external proscription (obedience).

Operational Interpretability

Pearlin and Kohn reason that jobs requiring self-direction lead to a positive evaluation of self-control and those requiring workers to follow the direction of an authority lead to a positive evaluation of obedience. Middle class jobs, they argue, are characterized by self-direction while working class jobs are characterized by following directions of authorities. The techniques used by the authors to measure self-direction and following directions are operational definitions necessary for testing their proposition.

To assess the effects of occupation the authors considered three occupational dimensions: (1) closeness of supervision, (2) principal type of work, and (3) self-reliance in work. Closeness of supervision was operationalized (measured) by three questionnaire items: (1) How much control does your direct supervisor exercise over your work? (2) Do you feel that you are able to make decisions about the things that have true importance to your work? (3) Do you have much influence on the way things go at your work? Consistent with the theoretical formulation, the more a worker feels he is controlled by his supervisor, the more likely he is to value obedience (according to the responses to the items in Table 5).

The principal type of work was divided into the components of things, people, or ideas. To assess these components, fathers were asked, "In almost all occupations it is necessary to work with ideas, people, and things, but occupations differ in the extent to which they require these types of activities. Considering now a typical day's work, which of these three aspects of work is most important in your occupation?" Consistent once again with their theoretical formulation, men selecting ideas as most important are more likely to value self-control, while men selecting things are more likely to value obedience.

The third occupational component, self-reliance in work, was measured by giving a list of qualities to fathers and asking them to rank order the three most important in terms of doing well at their work; and they were asked to distinguish among the remaining qualities those that were important or unimportant. Four items formed a self-reliance measure: (1) to understand one's self, (2) to be intelligent, (3) to have trust in one's self, and (4) to have a sense of responsibility. An index score was developed for each subject by giving a weight of 4 to an item ranked first, 3 if second, 2 if third, and 1 if considered important and unranked. The higher the self-reliance score (according to these four variables), the more likely men valued self-control and the lower the score, the more likely obedience was valued.

The use of questionnaire or interview items, such as these used by Pearlin and Kohn, illustrates one prevalent way of operationalizing concepts. An adequate operational concept has a specific well-defined meaning and is a reliable measure. Reliability, as stated previously, indicates that two or

Table 5.

Proportion of Parents in Italy and the United States Selecting Each Characteristic As One of the Three Most Important by Social Class

| | Italy | | | | United States | | | |
| | Fathers | | Mothers | | Fathers | | Mothers | |
Characteristic	Middle Class	Working Class	Middle Class	Working Class	Middle Class	Working Class	Middle Class	Working Class
1. Honesty	.54	.54	.55	.55	.52	.58	.44	.53
2. Good manners	.32*	.44*	.44	.51	.24	.25	.19	.24
3. Obedience to parents	.31*	.45*	.36*	.48*	.13*	.39*	.20*	.33*
4. Acts seriously	.25	.18	.18	.20	.00	.03	.00	.01
5. Self-control	.23*	.11*	.16*	.08*	.20*	.06*	.22*	.13*
6. Dependability	.23*	.13*	.21*	.10*	.33*	.08*	.24	.21
7. Ability to defend himself	.21	.14	.17*	.08*	.02*	.17*	.10	.06
8. Ambitiousness	.19	.17	.21	.19	.17	.08	.07	.13
9. Happiness	.14*	.07*	.16	.14	.37	.22	.46*	.36*
10. Consideration of others	.11	.09	.10*	.03*	.35*	.14*	.39*	.27*
11. Affectionate	.10	.12	.13	.12	.02	.08	.05	.04
12. Neatness and Cleanliness	.09	.14	.07*	.14*	.15	.17	.11*	.20
13. Popularity	.09	.07	.06	.04	.15	.25	.15	.18
14. Good student	.08*	.24*	.13*	.24*	.07	.19	.15	.17
15. Liked by adults	.04	.09	.05	.09	.00	.08	.05	.04
16. Curiosity	.03	.01	.02	.01	.13	.08	.18*	.06*
17. Ability to play by himself	.01	.02	.00	.01	.02	.06	.01	.02
Number of Cases	160	148	263	205	46	36	174	165

* Social Class difference statistically significant at the .05 level using chi-square test. For a discussion of statistical significance see pp. 111–113. Adapted from Leonard I. Pearlin and Melvin L. Kohn, "Social Class, Occupation, and Parental Values: A Cross-National Study," *American Sociological Review, 31* (August, 1966), p. 470.

more competent observers will get the same results or scores (within limits) when measuring the same phenomenon.

Although questions are often used by sociologists for operationalizing important concepts, reliable measurement (operational definitions) can be achieved through other observable means. As indicated in the section on observational techniques, such factors as height may be measured by position on a ruler, weight by a calibrated scale, speed by a stop watch, alienation by the number of people one talks to in a week period, socioeconomic status by gross yearly income, a "good salesman" by his actual monthly volume of sales, and the activity level of a seven year old by the frequency with which he wears out shoes.

The important point is that operational measures are readily interpretable. They do not yield several (and often competing) interpretations, because their meanings are not vague or incomprehensible. Operational measures, consequently, are crucial for an adequate understanding and interpretation of the information from social inquiries.

Communicability

The way concepts are operationally defined often determines their *level of measurement,* which in turn partially indicates the appropriate statistical manipulations (that is, data reduction techniques). The statistical manipulations form the basis for communicating the results of an empirical inquiry.

Level of measurement can be either qualitative or quantitative. Qualitative measurement distinguishes one class of objects from another—it does not specify the actual numerical differences between classes, and it does not rank order classes by specifying that one class is greater or less than another. Questionnaire items often, but not always, lead to qualitative measurement. Asking for an individual's religion, sex, or occupation yields qualitative distinctions because we are limited in saying only that two persons are different on these characteristics—we cannot say that females are greater than males, or Catholics are greater than Protestants, or parking lot attendants are twice as great as street car conductors. We are limited to such statements as "males are different from females," "Catholics are different from Protestants," and "parking lot attendants are different from street car conductors."

Quantitative measurement involves magnitude (greater or smaller amounts) and is illustrated by such characteristics as length, height, weight, the birth rate, family size, and income. There are four basic ways of achieving quantitative measurement: (1) direct enumeration (for example, counting the number of objects or persons in an area); (2) the use of a standard unit like the foot, the hour, and the pound; (3) using a "behavioral equivalent" that indicates a particular social phenomenon (for example, measuring alienation by the number of memberships in formal organizations or suicidal tendencies by the number or severity of personal accidents); and (4) ranking objects, such as contestants in a contest, or subjective measures of social class; for example, subjects placing themselves in the upper, middle, or lower class. Pearlin and Kohn's questionnaire items, which specifically define the three components of work (closeness of supervision, type of work, and self-reliance), lead to a ranking of objects. Some jobs, for example, require closer supervision than other jobs, but the exact amount of supervision is not measured. On this characteristic, consequently, jobs are rank ordered.

Once the measurement level is determined and the appropriate statistical techniques have been computed, the results need to be communicated so that unnecessary repetitious studies can be avoided and theories can be based on a wide range of findings. Results can be communicated by either describing the data at hand for the particular subjects in question (the sample) or inferring from such data to a larger group (the population). Descriptive statistics may include actual numbers, percentages, tables, or averages. To designate that group A has 20 members and group B has 10, for example, is to describe both groups on membership size. Inference statistics go beyond the data at hand (the sample) to estimate characteristics of the population from which the sample was drawn. Although the sample may be characterized by a murder rate of 9.2 per hundred thousand population and an average age of 24.6, the population it is supposed to represent may have a higher murder rate or a lower average age. There are inference techniques of reasonable accuracy for estimating population characteristics.

One of the handiest and most informative descriptive techniques is a statistical table. A table, like the one on the racial composition of churches in South Shore (Table 4), is one of the primary data reduction techniques. If properly labeled, a large amount of information can be presented in a small amount of space in a meaningful and ordered manner. A table may provide several meaningful comparisons that would otherwise require a large number of pages of verbal description. To illustrate, from Table 4 comparisons can be made between the Protestant and Catholic churches, or between the different Protestant denominations, or between blacks and whites in any particular denomination, or between membership and attendance for blacks or whites. From the information in the table, it can be determined that more blacks are in Catholic churches than Protestant; a Methodist church has the highest percentage black among the Protestant denominations; the percentage of black Sunday attenders is greater than the percentage of black memberships; and in some denominations, the percentage of blacks in Sunday school is much greater than the percentage of whites even though the denomination's membership is dominantly white. The large number and variety of comparisons illustrate the utility of a table as a data reduction technique and as a means for communicating information.

To obtain a clear notion of the nature of the information, the table, row, and column headings and the footnotes should be carefully checked. A table, usually, should be self-contained; that is, it should possess all the information necessary for its interpretation. Such information includes the nature of the sample and population, the location and time period in question, and the people who conducted the study.

Besides the table, there are a number of frequently used descriptive statistics that are useful summary measures of the data. Three very commonly used techniques are averages, dispersion of values, and relations between variables.

An average indicates the typical value or central tendency of a group of scores or numbers. To illustrate, the average IQ for a particular group may be 100; average height for the male population of a country may be five feet eight inches; and the average income for a census tract may be $14,000. Such averages have proved to be extremely important because they reduce the diverse data to one highly meaningful value that is easily grasped and communicated.

Sociologists usually use one of three different average measures or typical values: the *mode*, the *median*, and the arithmetic *mean*. The *mode* is simply the category (or categories) containing the highest frequency. The Methodist denomination is the model category for the number of blacks in Protestant Sunday schools (Table 4); and the modal proportion selecting obedience to parents as one of the three most important is working class mothers in Italy (Table 5).

The median is a different typical value that divides a distribution into two equal parts; it is the category or point above and below which 50 percent of the frequency lies. For example, if seven students have test scores as follows: two with 50 points, one with 70, one with 80, one with 90, and two with 100, the median score is 80. The mode in this case, however, is actually two scores (50 and 100), because these two scores are tied with the highest frequency of occurrence.

The mean is the arithmetic average and is defined as the sum of all the scores divided by their number. In the above example, first all test scores are added $(50+50+70+80+90+100+100=540)$; this sum is divided by the number of individuals, which is 7 $(540/7)$; the resulting value of 77.1 is the mean. Although the mean and the median are fairly close in value in the example, this is not a necessary result. The mean considers both the number of scores and the sums of their values in its computation, while the median is solely concerned with frequencies.

In general, the mean and median are considered superior to the mode as measures of average scores. Modal values are highly unstable (they may change drastically from one sample to the next), and they may change drastically even if only one individual score changes. Compared to the median (and the mode), the mean has two advantages: (1) it has a wider statistical application and (2) it is more stable in a sampling sense (the means from two random samples of the same population are more likely to be closer in value than two comparable medians). In certain types of problems, however, the median may have two advantages over the mean: (1) the median can be used on rank order data, while the mean is technically confined to more quantitative distributions and (2) the median is not as unduly affected as the mean by one or a few extreme scores.

Typical values are important descriptive measures, but considered alone, they can be misleading. Identical averages may represent two quite diverse distributions. To illustrate, suppose two groups have average IQ scores of 120. The first group could be characterized by individual IQ scores of 100, 110, 120, 130, and 140, while the second group may be comprised of five individual IQ scores of 120. Although they average the same, the second group is much less dispersed than the first. When evaluating a research study, consequently, it should be noted whether a dispersion measure is included along with a typical value or average.

To sum up to this point, three useful criteria for evaluating the communicability of results are the use of a tabular presentation (a table), and the presentation of both a dispersion measure and an average. These criteria, furthermore, are important descriptive data reduction techniques.

There are three widely used dispersion measures for particular problems: a range measure like the interquartile range, the average deviation, and the standard deviation. Interpretation of these measures may be found in standard introductory statistical texts.[10] It is important to note that dispersion measures indicate whether scores are tightly grouped about a particular value or if they are widely dispersed or spread out.

[10] See, for example, Labovitz and Hagedorn, footnote 1, *Introduction to Social Research,* and John H. Mueller, Karl F. Schuessler, and Herbert Costner, *Statistical Reasoning in Sociology,* Boston: Houghton Mifflin, 1970.

Briefly stated, the three dispersion measures have specific strengths and weaknesses. Any particular range measure considers only two scores in a distribution—*total range* is the highest score minus the lowest score, and the *interquartile range* is the score above which 25 percent of the cases lie minus the score below which 25 percent of the cases lie. The interquartile range, therefore, considers the spread only for the middle 50 percent of the cases. It is considered a more adequate dispersion measure than the total range, however, since in the latter case one deviantly high or low score can radically change the value of the dispersion measure.

To illustrate the difference between the total range and the interquartile range, consider the following distribution:

Educational Level Completed	Frequency
Grade 12	5
Grade 11	7
Grade 10	8
Grade 9	4
Grade 8	3
Grade 7	1

The total range for this distribution is 5 (12 minus 7), while the interquartile range, considering the middle fifty percent of the cases, is 1.96 (11.21 minus 9.25). If the one individual in Grade 7 was not in the sample, the total range would be 4 instead of 5. The change of this one individual would not have such a large effect on the interquartile range (a change from 1.96 to 1.81).

The *average deviation* and the *standard deviation* usually are superior techniques because they consider each score in a distribution. The distance of each score from an average value (the mean for the standard deviation and either the mean or the median for the average deviation) is the basic unit forming these dispersion measures. The average deviation, as the name implies, measures the average distance from the central value (mean or median) for each score. The standard deviation measures the square of the average distance from the central value. The standard deviation is used more often, of these two, because it forms the basis for more complex statistics, and with a particular kind of distribution (called the normal curve) it has a highly meaningful interpretation. The standard deviation, however, can be unduly influenced by one or a few extreme values (since all deviations are squared); in such cases the average deviation may be the most appropriate dispersion measure.

To illustrate these differences, consider again the distribution for educational level completed. The average deviation for the distribution is 1.09, while the standard deviation is 1.37. If we had found one more person with a completed education level of 20, the average deviation would change to 1.42, while the standard deviation would change to 2.25. This one extreme case, consequently, would have a larger effect on the standard deviation (a change of .88 as compared to .33).

Another frequently used set of descriptive statistical techniques are *association measures* for determining the relationship between two variables; these measures are based on the cross-tabulation of scores in two distributions. There are a large variety of measures of association, which are often based on different assumptions and are interpreted in quite different ways. (Discussion and interpretation of these measures are found in standard statistical texts.)

Relationship measures are extremely important statistical techniques in the social sciences. Research problems often hypothesize causal effects or relations from one variable to another. Race riots may be related to or caused by alienation; suicide by school or job-related tension; divorce by monetary problems; leadership by amount of knowledge or expertise; and child-rearing practices by size of community.

The selection of association measures ranges over several criteria. It is important to know the relevant criteria, because they are the rationales for the selection of one measure over another, and they provide the basis for judging their adequacy. It is beyond the scope of this chapter to discuss in detail the relative merits and deficiencies of all criteria, but it should be helpful for the evaluation of research studies to list and summarize those most frequently used.

An extremely important criterion for selecting a measure of association is understanding the *nature of the problem* in question. Does the theory indicate a correlation between variables (as one variable changes in value, so does another) or exact agreement (the exact values of one variable are predicted for another)? What is the logic of the hypotheses? For example, do they stipulate that changes in one variable cause changes in another or that changes in both variables are caused by some third variable? Are the hypotheses directional (predicting either an increase or decrease in values of a variable) or nondirectional (predicting only that the values of a variable will change but in an unknown direction)?

Answers to these questions actually describe and clarify the nature of the problem and narrow the selection of association measures. Although the nature of the problem is a primary criterion, there are other criteria that are useful in specifying finer distinctions in the selection process. Five such criteria are level of measurement, statistical assumptions, operational interpretation, retention of information, and form of the relation.

Level of measurement is perhaps the most frequently used criterion for selecting a measure of association. Certain measures are more appropriate for quantitative variables than for qualitative; and there are a few special measures for rankings or rank orders. The basic distinction between measures of association for quantitative and qualitative variables is based on two underlying principles—the principle of covariation and the principle of joint occurrence.

Covariation refers to relations between variables quantitatively measured, and applies to the case where a unit change in one is paralleled with some degree of regularity by a comparable change in another variable. That is, two variables somehow move together. Height, for example, is often directly related to weight, because taller people tend to weigh more than shorter people (but the relation is obviously not perfect); higher income persons tend to have more prestigious occupations; lower class people tend to have fewer material goods; the greater the leadership ability the more likely one is to be involved in community affairs; and the higher the IQ the greater the probability of success in college.

Two frequently used measures based on the principle of covariation are the correlation coefficient (r) and Spearman's rho (p) (which is used for rank order variables). Both measures yield a value between −1 and +1, where 0 indicates no relation between two variables and the two extremes indicate a perfect negative relation (−1) and a perfect direct relation (+1). If in all comparisons the taller person is always heavier than the shorter, then p would have a value of +1, which indicates a perfect direct relation between height and weight. If in all comparisons, however, the taller person is always lighter than the shorter, the p would have a value of −1, which indicates a perfect negative relation.

Measures of association based on the principle of joint occurrence are most often applied to qualitative variables. Joint occurrence refers to the idea that any unit, such as an individual, can be placed in several categories simultaneously. For example, an individual may be a rich male, a poor Catholic, an educated criminal, a brilliant writer, or a witty student. The relation is established by discovering if one category is frequently occupied by another category; for example, most airline pilots are male and most nurses are female (which suggests a relation between sex and occupation).

There are several measures of relation based on the principle of joint occurrence used for relating qualitative variables. Two frequently used measures are lambda and the coefficient of contingency (C). Both vary between 0 and +1, with 0 indicating no relation and +1 indicating the maximum relation. The value of lambda, for any particular relation between two variables, may be quite different depending on which variable is selected as dependent and which as independent. Lambda, consequently, is an asymmetrical measure (it yields two values for a cross-classification). C, in contrast, is symmetrical (it yields but one value, no matter which variable is selected as dependent or independent). If the specification of independent and dependent variables is important in the theoretical formulation, lambda should be selected over C.

Another important criterion for selecting measures of association is their *statistical assumptions.* To illustrate, some measures assume that there is meaningful order in the variable being related while others assume merely that clear conceptual distinctions can be made among the categories of variables, like distinguishing males from females or one occupation from another. As another illustration, interpretations of r assume that the variables are linearly related, so that when the cross-tabulated values of both variables are plotted they roughly form a straight line. If linearity cannot be assumed, then another measure, applicable to curvilinear data, should be selected to indicate the strength of relationship between two variables.

Operational interpretation is a farily frequently used criterion to select one measure of association over another. Measures with clear interpretations are more adequate than those without. For example, C is difficult to interpret in a precise manner, while r has several clear interpretations. It is useful to know the exact interpretations of each association measure to be able to adequately evaluate the relationships.

Another criterion is the *retention of information* in the data. Some measures utilize more of the characteristics of the data than do others. For example, if the knowledge of the differences between ordered observations is important, the correlation coefficient (r) should be selected over Spearman's rho (p). If individual A is eight inches taller than B, and B is two inches taller than C, the r value will reflect the magnitude of such differences, while the p value will only reflect that A is taller than B, and B is taller than C.

The last criterion considered is the *form of the relation,* which usually refers to the pictorial representation of the relation between variables. Two variables may be linearly or curvilinearly related—the former is represented by a straight line equation, while the latter can be represented by any number of curves. The relation between suicide and occupational prestige may be curvilinear in that the lowest and highest prestige occupations may have the highest rates. Consequently, in this case, as occupational prestige increases, the suicide rate starts high, then decreases, and then increases again. If the two variables were linearly and directly related then as occupational prestige increased so would the suicide rate. It is important to know the form of the relation, because if a straight line is fitted to curvilinear data, the magnitude and curvilinearity aspects of the relation would be missed.

In summary, six useful criteria for evaluating the selection of measures of association are (1) the nature of the problem, (2) level of measurement, (3) statistical assumptions, (4) operational interpretation, (5) retention of information, and (6) the form of the relation. If considered carefully, these criteria should help the student assess the adequacy of each measure of association for the problem in question.

So far only descriptive statistics for the sample have been considered in communicating results. Sociologists, however, often report inferential statistics, which are used to estimate the characteristics of the population from which the sample was drawn.

The proper use of inference statistics involves an adequately drawn random sample and a precisely designated population. Criteria for evaluating these two factors (representativeness and adequacy) were presented previously. In addition, the six criteria discussed for measures of association also apply, to some extent, to the use of inference statistics. That is, in evaluating the selection of inference statistics, the following should be considered: nature of the problem, measurement, assumptions, operational interpretation, information retention, and form of the relation.

It is important to note that the problem of inference is that of being able to say something about a population when you have data only from a sample. If 30 percent of a sample are married, what can we say about the percentage married in the population? Such inference is based on probability statements, which ultimately leads to a decision based on the budgeting of an error rate. That is, there is always an element of error in any conclusion based on inference statistics.

Based on probability, however, we can state what that risk of error is when trying to specify a population characteristic (percentage married) or when choosing between, say, two hypotheses. On the basis of inference statistics, we may be able to say that if 30 percent of the sample is married, then between 25 and 35 percent of the population is married; and the error in making this population inference is less than one percent. Stated differently, if we selected a large number of random samples from a population and made inferences on the percentage married, we may find that the inference is correct more than 99 times in 100.

To illustrate probability, consider an unbiased coin that is repeatedly and fairly tossed. The probability of either heads or tails is .50, that is, in the long run each event occurs about 50 percent of the time. Suppose we wanted to guess the outcome of two consecutive tosses rather than just one. The probability of being right is .25, that is, the probability of guessing correctly on the first toss and guessing correctly again on the second toss. If we tossed a coin twice, the possible outcomes are two heads, two tails, heads than tails, and tails then heads. Each of these four outcomes has a probability of occurring of .25.

Suppose a new coin was introduced and we wanted to determine whether it was biased. Suppose the person who introduced the coin bet you that he could guess the outcome of two consecutive tosses 75 percent of the time. You know that if it is an unbiased coin (fairly tossed), he will guess right only 25 percent of the time *in the long run.* If you bet him and lose all your money, then you should seriously consider two possibilities: (1) the probability in the long run is .25 and he was extremely lucky to guess correctly at a higher probability (for example, it is possible although highly unlikely to make 22 passes in a row at a dice table) or (2) the coin is biased in some way and you were cheated. Since there is a possibility that either outcome is correct (you never know for sure), you may be in error if you select one outcome over the other. You can reduce the error or risk of being wrong by observing many more tosses (you may also lose more money). The greater your adversary's success in taking your money and guessing right, the more likely he used a biased coin (or perhaps a biased toss). But it is possible although extremely remote that 100 or more correct guesses in a row occurred fairly.

If we believe an individual truly has ESP (extrasensory perception), we may ask him to predict certain outcomes such as which of two numbers or which of two cards was selected. If he is correct twice in a row we may say he has ESP, which is comparable to the conclusion of saying the coin is biased. But this could occur 25 percent of the time without ESP. The chance of guessing correctly twice in a row is so high (25 percent) that we would want more proof that the person truly has this mental ability.

Suppose, now, that he correctly guesses five times in a row. Would we be willing to say he has ESP? Comparing this case with that of an unbiased coin, correctly guessing the outcome of five consecutive tosses, on the basis of chance alone, occurs only about 3 percent of the time. At this point you may conclude that he has ESP, because there is small chance (only three times in a hundred) that he was correct by guessing alone.

If this is still too great a risk, we could give him more trials or opportunities to predict. At some point, however, we make a decision as to whether he does or does not have ESP. Since we cannot or do not test all cases, there is always some risk that we are wrong in our conclusions.

There are a variety of inference statistics that are used in sociology. Each one reflects the logic of the above examples of coin tossing and ESP. The most widely used inference statistics are called tests of significance (Table 5, page 100), which indicate (with an element of risk) whether two or more variables are related in a nonzero way in a population, or whether an experimental variable or stimulus has an effect, or whether a characteristic of a sample is reasonably close (within chance fluctuations) to the population characteristic.

Analysis of variance, student's t, chi square, Fisher's exact probability test, and the Mann-Whitney U test perhaps are mostly used in sociology. The student should consult standard statistical texts for the interpretations of these and other inference statistics.

SUMMARY

The criteria for evaluating data analysis techniques can be subsumed under (1) the theoretical formulation, (2) operational interpretability, and (3) communicability. Adequate data analysis is closely tied to the researcher's theory or ideas and the general nature of the problem in question. In general, the closer an analysis is to the theoretical formulation, the more sense it makes and the more readily its importance can be evaluated. Operational interpretations are important for they yield relatively clear and comprehensible results. Without such interpretations, the data may be interpreted in several conflicting ways and, consequently, the results of the study would be vague. Finally, the results of the study must be communicated to others in a comprehensible manner. Communicability is enhanced by the use of adequate statistical techniques like tables, averages, dispersion measures, relationship measures, and inference procedures.

Theoretical formulation, operational interpretability, and communicability are closely interrelated. The theory is essential for interpreting and communicating data in a clear and comprehensive way. Operational measures, furthermore, are important forerunners to the adequate communication of results. If variables have several meanings or rather loosely formulated meanings, then the results of the study will be unclear and, consequently, difficult to communicate.

Epilogue

We have attempted to provide the reader with an introduction and some insight into the nature of sociology. The subject matter of sociology has been depicted as rather broad in scope—it includes the structural components of society as well as social interaction and the interpretation of individual motives. The field reflects the growth of contemporary society, as evidenced by the substantive concerns and emotional tone of the orientations of radical and black sociology. Despite the important changes, the core ideas of sociology may be tied to the past and to significant founding fathers—Durkheim, Weber, and Simmel.

The members of the sociological discipline, however, are not in complete agreement on either the nature of its subject matter or on the scientific techniques for social inquiry. Specifically, dissensus characterizes sociologists with regard to its proper domain of study (structure, interaction, or motives), and with regard to the appropriate nature of scientific evidence and explanation (functionalism, *Vestehen,* or positivism).

Such disagreement over establishing and explaining

scientific facts and over the proper domain of sociology does not appear to be having an adverse effect on the growth of the field. Perhaps to some extent sociology has been viable and important because of the controversies, which has led to serious debate and empirical investigations. Debate and investigations, in turn, are important factors in the changing nature of sociology, which has been evident in recent times.

Besides the dominant substantive and scientific orientations in sociology, some commonly used techniques and methods in carrying out and analyzing studies were presented. The ability to evaluate studies is important because such research forms the basis for established knowledge in the field.

How sociologists view the content of their field (substantive orientations), how they view evidence and explanation (scientific orientations), and how they carry out social research are critical elements in understanding the nature of sociology. They are not the only elements, however. A larger treatise would consider the explanatory and descriptive nature of the important sociological concepts pertaining to behavior and action. Being a rather modest scientific discipline in terms of established knowledge, an introduction to its concepts may be the next most important means of understanding the nature of sociology, after learning about its orientations and methods. Some of its major concepts are norms, values, status, roles, power, authority, stratification, and social class. The various orientations in sociology approach these concepts in different ways and emphasize the importance of some over others.

SOCIOLOGY AS A DYNAMIC DISCIPLINE

Sociology is constantly in a state of change or fluctuation. Newly formulated concepts, newly established scientific facts, new methods for social inquiry, and new perspectives have reflected a changing social world.

The concepts of sociology undergo continual scrutiny and change. They have changed substantially in the past; they are currently in the process of change; and they will undoubtedly change in the future. An active and viable discipline is characterized by such change.

The definitions of existing concepts in sociology may be too vague in meaning, or too limited or broad in scope, or lead to imprecise measurement. Concomitant with the growth of any science, consequently, is a change in its concepts; and depending on the problem, the theoretical orientation, and research findings, the scientist often takes an active part in their reconceptualization. This active role may lead to theoretical and empirical innovations that result in verified propositions.

Whereas older sociological investigations stressed such concepts as social class, some current inquiries are based on a reconceptualization and use the more specific concept of socioeconomic status (SES) in differentiating among individuals and social groups. SES is more conceptually useful (being based on measurable dimensions of prestige, income, and education) and is more readily observable. It is more specific than the general and vague concept of social class. Religiosity too has changed from a conceptualization based on a vague feeling about God and church to explicit underlying dimensions—for example, ideology (can God will the end of the world?), ritual (must people go to church?), and experience (does religion give purpose to life?). As concepts lose their utility in the contemporary scene, they are either discarded or modified.

Scientific facts have changed the nature of sociology by suggesting new concepts and theories. The discovery that certain people felt there were more babysitters in their new residence area (when there were actually considerably less) led to the idea of social trust as a significant factor in perception. In the perception of the number of potential babysitters in an area, the actual number proved to be less important than the structure of interpersonal relations. The fact that feelings of satisfaction with army life were not very different between United States soldiers overseas and those remaining at home, led to the notion of relative deprivation. Rather than comparing themselves to each other, it seemed that soldiers overseas compared themselves to those in combat, and those at home compared themselves to those overseas; consequently, neither group felt too deprived. The discovery that bystanders or witnesses to certain events (a man being robbed, a woman being raped, or a child being beaten) will more likely help if they are alone rather than in the midst of a crowd questions the current widespread belief that modern man is alienated from society and does not want to get involved. Rather than alienation, the sheer number of witnesses may be the important variable in whether the victim will receive immediate aid. The relatively high rate of drug usage among medical doctors negates the preconceived idea that such usage is strictly a lower-class phenomena. These illustrations and a large variety of other social facts have proved to be a dominant influence in the changing character of sociology.

The development of new methods for investigation has led to a changing sociology, primarily because they often lead to the discovery of important facts and relations. The development of a physical apparatus called an interaction machine for the recording of the number and lengths of inter- actions (among other uses) has led to important notions about leaders, isolates, and the communication patterns in small groups. Multivariate statistical techniques and the use of modern day computers have permitted more detailed and extensive analysis of social phenomena. Such techniques enhance the simultaneous use of several intricate variables, thereby permitting the development of complex and realistic theories about the social order.

Finally, new orientations have contributed to the changing nature of sociology by challenging its traditional assumptions about human behavior, pointing out conflicting ideas, and to some degree presenting a new way to view social pheno- mena. Radical and black sociology are clear examples of this factor. Their advocates have challenged sociology on being a value-free discipline and have stressed the usage of certain concepts over others (black over Negro, racism over discrimination, and conflict over competition). Ethnome- thodology also has challenged some of the traditional notions of sociology by emphasizing the study of the routine activities of people's everyday lives, and by questioning the utility of some widely used research techniques.

SOCIOLOGY AND THE STUDENT

At this point you might think you have just about finished another book you can quickly forget. We hope this is not the case, and we strongly urge you not to discard the major ideas presented, such as substantive and scientific orientations and methods of research. We believe that in at least three ways, the contents of this book and of sociology in general can be important to you by: (1) providing new ways of looking at and understanding the world around you, (2) providing a body of knowledge about social life in general, and (3) preparing you for further education and an occupation.

The orientations in sociology, although somewhat conflicting and diverse, do provide different ways of viewing human events. Rather than taking our old point of view or even just one, we have several at our disposal; and each may give us some insight into the nature of social interaction and behavior. Knowledge of the social structure and of the characteristics of the social interactions and motivations occurring in a person's life may permit us to understand why some people use drugs, commit suicide, hate blacks, or dislike foreigners.

The orientations of sociology not only permit an individual to gain some insight into why he is what he is today, but why others are what they are. Such understanding may lead to cooperation, better forms of communication, and more desirable interpersonal feelings about one another. The understanding that may accrue in applying sociological orientations to personal problems and social problems may eventually lead to the solution of some.

In relating our values to the social world, one important question is: why is man so inhumane to man? Stated more specifically, why is there so much war, conflict, racism, discrimination, prejudice, hunger, poverty and, in general, human misery? Now try to apply the sociological orientations to such inhumanity and see if you can gain some insights into the problem.

As a body of knowledge, we have alluded to the fact that sociology must be considered a rather modest science. We have no sociological equivalents for exploding bombs or sending spacecraft to the moon or elsewhere. But the discipline is far from complete ignorance. Many thousands of empirical studies have produced innumerable facts about social life. We cannot make universal statements such as all upper income people have small families, or all people in highly prestigious occupations belong to and participate in community associations. We can state, however, that there is some probability that as income per family increases, family size decreases; and there is a greater probability that persons in more prestigious occupations will belong to and participate in community associations more than those in less prestigious occupations. Such a body of knowledge, if used judiciously, can help us to understand and interpret our social worlds.

Finally, sociological knowledge provides a useful preparation for further education and an occupation. An understanding of modern societies and other types of social groups is almost a necessary condition for graduate work in any of the social sciences and humanities. It certainly cannot hurt as part of a well-rounded background.

Besides education, there are a variety of jobs where an understanding of people and the way they behave is a definite asset. In fact, any job that is not in complete isolation would benefit from such understanding by aiding us in getting along with co-workers. Some jobs, however, seem to be more attuned to sociological orientations than others—for example, social welfare, teaching, counsellors, recreation workers, administrative assistants, and research assistants.

In many ways, sociology can be of value to you as it has been to the authors. If, as we hope, many of you take other courses in sociology, a knowledge of its orientations and methods should prove to be a sound background.

Glossary

The following definitions are consistent with their usage in the text. Some of the definitions include concepts that are defined elsewhere in the glossary. Adequate use of the glossary may require cross-referencing (for example, in looking up "cause" you may want to check the definition of "rationale"). It should prove useful, furthermore, to check the index for the pages on which the concepts are discussed. These pages often provide examples and detailed descriptions.

Adequacy of Sample–The sample is of sufficient size to permit a specified confidence in inferences made to the population.

Alienation–Personal feelings or objective measures of powerlessness, meaninglessness, self-estrangement, or isolation.

Association–The statistical relation between two or more variables, either by covariation or joint occurrence. Variables may change in conjunction with one another, or they jointly occur with some regularity.

Average Deviation–The mean or median differences (deviations) of all scores in a distribution. The absolute sum of all differences divided by the number of individuals.

Behavioral Interaction Orientation–A substantive perspective based on the study of behavioral interaction patterns among individuals, that is, the patterns of reciprocal give and take between two or more persons, or the overt (observable) patterns of behavior occurring in interpersonal relations.

Black Sociology–A recently developed perspective, which stresses relevance and moral evaluations and works for the betterment of black people. Black sociologists oppose the existing "establishment" white sociologists, have a radical political orientation, and employ a conflict model of society (based on the racial distinction between whites and blacks).

Case Study–The observation of one unit (population or sample) at one point in time.

Cause–A variable is considered a cause of another variable if it satisfies the criteria of (1) a nonzero association, (2) time priority, (3) nonspuriousness, and (4) rationale (theory).

Completeness of a Population–Refers to the extent to which a population list contains all the individuals or units of interest.

Control Group–The group in an experiment that is observed, but not subjected to the experimental variable (stimulus).

Correlation Coefficient *(r)*–A measure of the degree of relation based on the principle of covariation used with quantitative variables.

Covariation–For quantitative data, the situation where a unit change in one variable is paralleled with some degree of regularity by a comparable change in another variable; for example, height and weight or education and income.

Cross-classification–A frequency distribution based on the simultaneous tabulation of the categories of two or more variables.

Data Reduction–Grouping information into a few categories or computing a small number of statistics to adequately describe the characteristics of a sample or population.

Dependent Variable–The effect that is caused by the independent variable; also, the variable that you are trying to explain or predict.

Descriptive Statistics—Techniques and measures indicating the characteristics of the data at hand—for example, frequency distributions, typical values, dispersion, and relations.

Dispersion (variation, scatter)–The amount of spread or differences among the scores of a distribution.

Dysfunctional–A part lessens the adjustment of the system or is maladaptive for the system.

Ecological Perspective–A structural orientation based on the study of societal factors such as technology, natural resources, and demographic composition (population size and density, sex ratio, family size, fertility, mortality, and migration patterns).

Empirical–Subject to observation through the senses.

Equilibrium–Within the functional orientation it refers to the tendency for a system to achieve a balance among its parts.

Ethnomethodology–A recently developed perspective concerned with the study of (1) the methods people use to carry out their everyday activities, (2) language and meanings, and (3) the normative aspects of situations.

Evidence, Scientific–Criteria used to establish scientific facts. Criteria vary depending on the perspectives of *Verstehen* or positivism. Evidence is established by plausibility and estheticism (**Verstehen**) or by observation and verifiability (positivism).

Experimental Design–Generally based on a small number of individuals and often carried out in a controlled environment to reduce the effects of unknown factors. The stimulus is usually carefully controlled by the researcher and administered to only one group (experimental), and withheld from another (control).

Experimental Group–The group in an experiment comprised of individuals or units receiving the experimental variable (stimulus).

Frequency Distribution—The separation of a variable into mutually exclusive classes and the number of individuals in each class.

Functional–A part contributes to the adjustment of the system.

Functional Equivalents—A need of a system can be met by a variety of equally adequate functional alternatives.

Functional Orientation–A scientific perspective designating that social and psychological phenomena are explained by the purpose they serve. The goal of functionalism is to demonstrate the contribution or the maladaptation of the parts of the system for the whole.

Group Structure Perspective–A structural orientation based on the study of the form or makeup of social groups (that is, interdependent individuals with an identity). The form includes the communication system, authority structure, group size, power, and the division of labor.

Heterogeneity of a Population–The extent to which the units or individuals in question are different.

Historical Evidence–The use of either secondary data sources such as census reports and vital statistics, or the personal accounts of historians, travelers, or other such writers. Its general meaning refers to written records of past events.

Hypothesis–A testable statement asserting the relationship between two or more variables under stated conditions.

Independent Variable–The predictive, explanatory, or causal variable that occurs, or is assumed to occur, prior to the effect or dependent variable.

Inference Statistics–Techniques used to estimate population characteristics from sample data.

Interaction, Social–The reciprocal influence exerted by two or more persons on one another. The behavior of one individual produces a response in another individual.

Interquartile Range–Dispersion measure that gives the distance (range) encompassing the middle 50 percent of the scores in a distribution.

Interview–The situation in which answers are elicited from respondents by a person who asks for and usually records responses.

Joint Occurrence–For qualitative data, the situation where individuals can be placed in several categories simultaneously: for example, "male" and "delinquent" or "easy" and "professor."

Level of Measurement–Variables may be qualitatively or quantitatively determined (measured).

Mean–The arithmetic average, which is the sum of all the scores divided by their number.

Measurement–The assignment, according to rules, of numbers or other symbols to categories or classes.

Median–The category or value above and below which 50 percent of the total frequency lies; or the middle category dividing the distribution into two equal parts.

Mode–The category (or categories) containing the highest frequency in a distribution.

Motivation–As used in the text, it refers to a subjective intention underlying an individual's action. Motivations are an important part of the social action orientation. In general, it refers to the regulation of need-satisfying and goal-seeking behavior.

Network of Interdependent Positions Perspective–A structural orientation based on the study of positions or statuses that are viewed as independent of any individual. Persons carry out the duties and obligations that are attached to their position and interact with those in other positions.

Nonfunctional–The part is irrelevant to the adjustment of the system.

Nonspurious Relation–A situation in which the relation between two or more variables cannot be explained by other variables.

Normative Structure Perspective–A structural orientation based on the study of the standards of conduct that influence persons in their behavioral and thought patterns. Such standards of conduct refer to the rules, laws, and customs of the members of societies and other social groups.

Operational Definition–The measurement or observational procedure is clearly specified so that competent observers will obtain the same results when measuring the same phenomenon. It also refers to the specification of the procedures that are necessary for identifying the concept in question.

Panel Study–Repeated observations of the same sample or population over a period of time.

Participant Observation–Includes a broad range of techniques such as (1) interacting in the field with subjects, (2) direct observations of behavior, (3) interviewing, and (4) relatively few restrictions on the researcher. The researcher may act as or be a member of the group he is studying.

Population–The largest number of individuals or units of interest to the researcher. Results of the study are inferred to the population.

Positivistic Orientation–A scientific orientation designating that a fact is established by reliable and verifiable observations, and facts are explained by subsuming them under causal laws. Its general meaning refers to the use of the scientific method (as in the physical sciences) for the study of phenomena. In sociology, positivism is based on the assumption that social and physical phenomena can be studied by similar techniques.

Precision of a Population–The degree to which a population is well-defined (operational).

Prediction–A statement about the expected values of a variable not yet observed that is based on the knowledge of values of other variables. Sometimes used to refer to a quantitative statement concerning a relation between two or more variables.

Psychological Functionalism–A functional explanation where the level of analysis is the individual.

Qualitative–Distinguishing one class of objects from another type or kind rather than by magnitude, as for example, in distinguishing Catholics from other religious groups.

Quantitative–Measurement of variables in terms of magnitude, extent, or amount, such as height, weight, and population size.

Questionnaire–An instrument used in social inquiries comprised of a series of questions that are filled in by the respondent himself.

Radical Sociology–A recently developed perspective, which stresses relevance and moral evaluations, and works for the betterment of the alienated and the poor in society. Radical sociologists oppose the existing "establishment" sociologists, have a radical (left) political orientation, and usually employ a conflict model of society.

Random Sample, Simple–Each individual in a defined group has an equal chance of being chosen, and the selection of any one individual has no effect on the selection of any other.

Range, Total–The highest minus the lowest scores in a distribution.

Ranking–Establishing classes of a variable into greater than or less than other classes on a selected dimension; for example, on prestige, professional occupations are ranked higher than manual occupations.

Rationale–Statements logically justifying the relation between two or more variables.

Recentness of a Population–Refers to the extent to which a population list is contemporary (and therefore accurate) or out-of-date.

Regression Effects–The tendency of extreme scores to be less extreme in a subsequent period of observation; they regress toward the mean.

Relation (see Association)

Reliability–The condition in which repeated observations of the same phenomena with the same instrument yield similar results.

Replication–The repetition of an empirical study.

Representativeness of Design–The utilization of realistic situations. As opposed to contrived situations, these are assumed to indicate how people actually respond in their everyday lives.

Representativeness of Sample–The degree to which the part (sample) reflects the characteristics of the population.

Role–The performance of an individual in carrying out the social expectations, rules, and regulations associated with a specific position. The role of student may include taking notes, participating in discussions, reading assigned materials, and studying for and taking examinations. Also role is frequently defined as the norms attached to a position.

Role-taking–In general, the process of putting oneself in the other person's place. Specifically, a process in which persons become human by learning the social roles (expectations, rules, and regulations) of society, by placing themselves in the roles of others.

Sample–A part of a population. Often knowledge of that part forms the basis for inferring characteristics about a population.

Sampling Bias–The degree to which a sample does not accurately reflect the characteristics of the population, which it was drawn to represent.

Sampling Error–Unrepresentativeness of a population due to random fluctuations.

Scientific Explanation–Criteria used to establish the relationships between scientific facts. Criteria varies depending on the perspectives of *Verstehen,* functionalism, or positivism. Explanation is established by motives (*Verstehen*), purpose (functionalism), or subsuming a fact or relation under a scientific law (positivism).

Scientific Law–A hypothesis that has been repeatedly supported by empirical tests (which satisfy the criteria of a nonzero association, time priority of the independent variable, nonspuriousness, and rationale).

Scientific Method, Positivistic–A body of procedures for discovering the conditions under which events occur, generally characterized by verifiability, operational definitions, and empirical observation.

Scientific Orientation–A perspective, point of view, or frame of reference, specifying the nature of acceptable evidence and/or the nature of an acceptable explanation. The three major scientific orientations in sociology are functionalism, *Verstehen,* and positivism

Sensitization–The process of making subjects aware of factors in the study that changes their responses.

Social Action–Human behavior that is subjectively meaningful, or behavior that is motivated.

Social Action Orientation–A substantive perspective based on the study of behavior that is subjectively meaningful to the persons involved.

Social Exchange Theory–A subtype of the behavioral interaction orientation, which is based on an operant conditioning (stimulus-response), psychological model, and a rational economic model. Its major proposition is that every human interaction is an exchange of goods, services, or sentiments.

Socialization–The process of transmitting a group's norms, values, beliefs, attitudes, and behavioral patterns to newcomers. Conversely, a process by which a person develops self-awareness and identity, and learns to operate competently in his social environment.

Social Norm–A standard of conduct that specifies what one should or should not do. These standards may have positive or negative sanctions attached to them (that is, rewards or punishments).

Social Status–A group position. Often such positions have differential prestige.

Social Stratification–A hierarchical ranking of groups or individuals based on criteria such as social class, occupation, power, and prestige.

Social Structure–Factors that are persistent over time and are external to the individual (like technology, urbanization, and social norms) and are assumed to influence behavior and thought.

Social Survey–A design involving a rather large sample of a population or a selected segment; it is usually associated with the data gathering technique of the questionnaire or interview.

Social Values–Desired ends or goals, or general conceptions of the desirable.

Sociology–The scientific or systematic study of human conduct utilizing the perspectives of human interaction, social action, and social structure.

Spatial Control–Achievement, by matching and randomization, of pretest equality between experimental and control groups.

Split-half Reliability–If test questions or questionnaire items are theoretically assumed to be measuring similar phenomena, then half of the items (first half or odd numbers) may be correlated with the remaining half (second half or even numbers). A high correlation indicates a reliable instrument.

Standard Deviation–A measure of the dispersion of scores from the mean of a distribution. It is the square root of the averaged squared differences (deviations) from the mean.

Standard Unit–An established dimension by which units are measured, such as the foot, the hour, or the pound.

Stratified Random Sample–Separate random samples are taken from theoretically important categories of the population (such as from upper, middle, and lower income groups).

Structural Functionalism–A functional explanation where the level of analysis is structural.

Structural Orientation–A substantive perspective based on the study of the structural components of groups—that is, external social factors that are assumed to influence the behavior of individuals and groups. The structural orientation subsumes the four related perspectives labeled ecological, network of interdependent positions, group structure, and normative structure.

Substantive Orientation–A perspective, point of view, or frame of reference, specifying the major parts of the world that are important by indicating the content relevant for study. The three major substantive orientations in sociology are structural, social action, and behavioral interaction.

Symbolic Interaction Orientation–A subtype of the social action orientation, which emphasizes the study of language and gesture as crucial aspects of human communication and socialization. This perspective assumes that an individual's self-identity and society's structure are products of interaction between symbolically communicating human beings.

Table–An ordered arrangement of numerical data placed in rows and columns, with concise labels specifying the nature of the data.

Temporal Control–Elimination of the effects of extraneous factors occurring between the pretest and posttest by use of a control group.

Test of Significance–An inference technique usually used to indicate whether two or more variables are related in a non-zero way in a population, or whether an experimental variable has an effect, or whether a characteristic of a sample is reasonably close to a population characteristic.

Time Priority–One variable occurs first or changes prior to another variable.

Typical Value (central tendency)–The average score or most frequently counted category of a variable: for example, the median, the mean, or the mode.

Validity–A technique that measures a variable's theoretically defined dimension—it measures what it is supposed to measure.

Verifiability–A conclusion or factual statement can be subjected to more than one observation or test.

Verstehen **Orientation**–A scientific orientation designating that a fact is established by plausibility and estheticism, and facts are explained by establishing the motives or subjective meanings of individuals. It stresses an empathy of the subject and the situation by the social investigator. Adequate explanation or understanding is determined by the satisfaction a scientist derives from his interpretation of an event.

Index